Understanding Economics for NCEA Level Three: Micro-economic concepts TR
1st Edition
Dan Rennie

Typeset by *Book*NZ

Any URLs contained in this publication were checked for currency during the production process. Note, however, that the publisher cannot vouch for the ongoing currency of URLs.

Acknowledgements
Thank you to the following who assisted in various ways to make this publication possible:
- my family - Sue, Nicole, Jacob and Brooke.
- Jane for her typing
- Sally for proof reading

For product information and technology assistance,
in Australia call **1300 790 853**;
in New Zealand call **0800 449 725**

For permission to use material from this text or product, please email
aust.permissions@cengage.com

National Library of New Zealand Cataloguing-in-Publication Data
Rennie, Dan, 1959-
Understanding economics NCEA level three. Micro-economic concepts teacher resource / Dan Rennie.
ISBN 978-017024-122-9
1. Economics—Study and teaching (Secondary) I. Title.
330.0712—dc 23

Cengage Learning Australia
Level 7, 80 Dorcas Street
South Melbourne, Victoria Australia 3205

Cengage Learning New Zealand
Unit 4B Rosedale Office Park
331 Rosedale Road, Albany, North Shore 0632, NZ

For learning solutions, visit **cengage.com.au**

Printed in China by RR Donnelley Asia Printing Solutions Limited.
1 2 3 4 5 6 7 16 15 14 13 12

CONTENTS

PREFACE

Demonstrate understanding of micro-economic concepts is a stand-alone text and workbook designed to cover aspects of Achievement Standard 3.3.

1 UTILITY

Key concepts and terms: the law of diminishing marginal utility, the optimal purchase rule and consumer equilibrium, intuitive derivation of individual demand curves using marginal utility. (3.3)

UTILITY AND DEMAND

Tony Gordon's utility schedule for chewing gum each day		
Quantity consumed (packs)	Total utility (TU) (cents)	Marginal utility (MU) (cents)
1	80	80
2	144	64
3	192	48
4	224	32
5	244	20
6	244	0
7	230	−14

Tony Gordon's demand schedule for chewing gum each day	
Price (cents)	Quantity demanded (packs)
80	1
64	2
48	3
32	4
20	5
0	6

As people consume goods or services they gain satisfaction (termed utility). **Marginal utility (MU)** is the change or additions to total utility resulting from consumption of one extra unit of a good or service. **Total utility (TU)** is the aggregate satisfaction gained from consuming successive quantities of a good.

As more of a product is consumed (as shown in the table), total satisfaction (total utility) increases but this will be at a decreasing rate. This is known as the **law of diminishing marginal utility**, that is, as more of a good or service is consumed holding all else constant, total utility increases but at a decreasing rate.

From the table we can observe that if a consumer's purchases increase, then the MU will decrease. Therefore if a consumer was to decrease his or her purchases of a product, then MU would increase.

The rational consumer attempting to maximise his or her total utility should purchase more goods until price **(P) equals MU**; this is the **optimum purchase rule**. The individual demand curve is therefore derived from the individual's MU curve, that is, because consumers receive less extra satisfaction as consumption increases they will only buy more if the price falls.

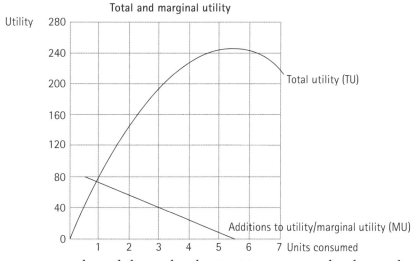

From the graph we can see that while total utility is rising, marginal utility is always positive but beyond the point when total utility is maximised, marginal utility becomes negative. When total utility is at a maximum, marginal utility is zero.

ISBN 9780170241212
ISBN 9780170241229

EQUI-MARGINAL RULE (A THEORY)

For a consumer aiming to maximise total satisfaction and achieve consumer equilibrium they must satisfy these conditions:

1 spend all their income and
2 the marginal utility per dollar must be equal

i.e., $\dfrac{MUa}{\text{price a}} = \dfrac{MUb}{\text{price b}} = \dfrac{MUc}{\text{price c}}$

In this situation the consumer equilibrium is achieved because the marginal utility of the last dollar spent on each good or service is equal.

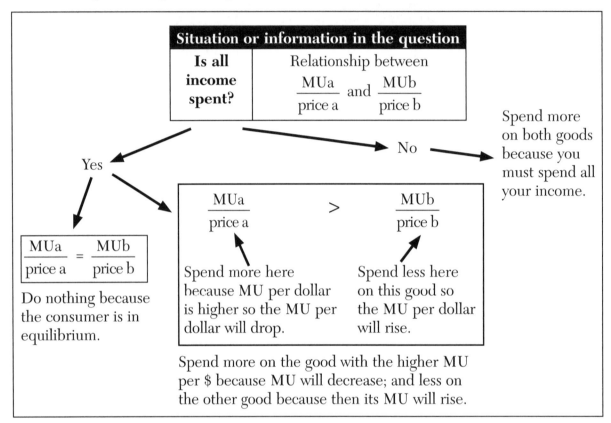

For example, Rangi has $200 to spend and buys 15 of 'x' at $6 and considers the MU of 'x' to be 30. He buys 10 of 'y' at $11 and considers the MU of 'y' to be 55. How can he maximise his total satisfaction?

1 Has Rangi spent all his $200 income?   Yes
   because   15 of 'x' at $6 =   90
   and   10 of 'y' at $11 =   110
                                          $ 200

2 Does $\dfrac{MUa}{\text{price a}} = \dfrac{MUb}{\text{price b}}$? Yes

   because $\dfrac{30}{6} = \dfrac{55}{11}$

   i.e. $5 = 5$

Rangi has satisfied the conditions to maximise satisfaction, he should do nothing.

If Sam purchased the same quantities as Rangi and considered the marginal utilities of the products to be the same but had $220 to spend, he has not maximised his satisfaction because he has not spent all his income, so must spend more on both goods.

Maria has $50 to spend and buys 20 of 'a' at $1 and 15 of 'b' at $2. She considers the MU of 'a' to be 8 and the MU of 'b' to be 12. She meets the first condition of spending all her income of $50 but her MU per dollar are not equal.

Maria has spent all her $50 income because: 20 of 'a' at $1 = $20
15 of 'b' at $2 = $30
$50

Does $\dfrac{MUa}{\text{price a}} = \dfrac{MUb}{\text{price b}}$? No

$\left(\dfrac{8}{1} \neq \dfrac{12}{2} \right)$

Maria should buy more of 'a' since it has the higher MU per dollar and less of 'b'.

ISBN 9780170241212
ISBN 9780170241229

KEY TERMS AND IDEAS

Utility means satisfaction Consumers aim to maximise total satisfaction As more cans are consumed the MU decreases	Zoe's utility schedule for cans of drink (per day)			Zoe's demand schedule for cans of drink (per day)	
	Cans consumed	Total utility (cents)	Marginal utility (cents)	Price (cents)	Quantity demanded (cans)
	1	100	100	100	1
	2	180	80	80	2
	3	230	50	50	3
	4	240	10	10	4

Law of diminishing marginal utility	As more of a good/service is consumed, the total utility will increase at a decreasing rate (i.e., marginal utility will decrease).
Optimum purchase rule	A consumer desiring to maximise total utility should purchase more goods and services until price equals marginal utility (P = MU).
Explaining why MU leads to the downwards sloping demand curve	As consumption increases, MU decreases. The rational consumer attempting to maximise his/her satisfaction will be prepared to purchase to where P = MU. Consumers will only purchase additional units at a lower price. The individual demand curve is therefore derived from the individual MU curve.
Equi-marginal rule Consumer equilibrium is reached when marginal utility of the last dollar spent on each commodity is equal	(a) (i) must spend all income and (ii) $\dfrac{MU_a}{price\ a} = \dfrac{MU_b}{price\ b}$ Solution: Do nothing (b) Not all income spent Spend more on both goods (c) all income spent $\dfrac{MU_a}{price\ a} \neq \dfrac{MU_b}{price\ b}$ Spend more on good with higher MU per \$ and less on other good
Total utility (TU)	The aggregate satisfaction gained from consuming successive quantities of a good.
Marginal utility (MU)	The change in total utility resulting from the consumption of one extra unit of a given commodity.

ISBN 9780170241212
ISBN 9780170241229

STUDENT NOTES: UTILITY

Utility – means satisfaction, consumers aim to maximise satisfaction. The table below shows that as more units are consumed the marginal utility (MU) decreases. If the price of a product rises there will be a resulting decrease in the amount purchased and an increase in the MU as a result.

Units consumed	Total utility (cents)	Marginal utility (cents)
1	500	500
2	900	400
3	1 000	100
4	1 050	50

Demand schedule using MU	
Price (cents)	Quantity demanded
500	1
400	2
100	3
50	4

Total utility (TU)   The aggregate satisfaction gained from consuming successive quantities of a good.

Marginal utility (MU)   The change in total utility resulting from the consumption of one extra unit of a given commodity.

Explaining why MU leads to the downward-sloping demand curve.   As consumption increases, MU decreases. The rational consumer attempting to maximise his/her satisfaction will be prepared to purchase to where P = MU. Consumers will only purchase additional units at a lower price. The individual demand curve is therefore derived from the individual MU curve.

Optimum purchase rule   A consumer desiring to maximise total utility should purchase more goods and services until price equals marginal utility.

Equi-marginal rule   Consumer equilibrium is reached when marginal utility of the last dollar spent on each commodity is equal, it requires that all income is spent and that the
$$\frac{MUa}{price\ a} = \frac{MUb}{price\ b}$$

The law of diminishing marginal utility – As more of a good or service is consumed, the total utility will increase at a decreasing rate.

ISBN 9780170241212
ISBN 9780170241229

PRACTISE QUESTIONS AND TASKS

1 a Explain the difference between total utility and marginal utility.

Total utility is the aggregate satisfaction gained from consuming successive quantities of a good.

Marginal utility is the change in total utility resulting from the consumption of a given commodity.

MU = TU2 – TU1

b Explain the law of diminishing marginal utility.

As more of a good/service is consumed, the total utility will increase at a decreasing rate (i.e. MU will

fall) or successive equal additions to consumption result in smaller amounts of extra utility.

c Complete the table that shows Ian's total and marginal utility from buying cans of soft drink per week.

Quantity consumed (cans)	Total utility (cents)	Marginal utility (cents)
1	200	200
2	360	160
3	460	100
4	524	64
5	564	40

d Use the concept of marginal utility to explain why the demand curve for the product slopes downward.

As consumption increases, the marginal utility gained by consuming the product will fall. As the

marginal utility falls, a rational consumer will be less willing to make the same sacrifice to buy the

goods/producers will only sell more by reducing price.

e Use the information in the table above to complete Ian's demand schedule for cans of soft drink per week and draw a demand curve in the grid provided.

Ian's demand schedule for cans of soft drink per week	
Price (cents)	Quantity demanded
200	1
160	2
100	3
64	4
40	5

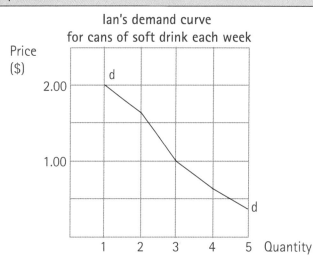

Ian's demand curve for cans of soft drink each week

2 **a** Complete the table and use it to complete the sentences.

Quantity consumed (pies)	Total utility	Marginal utility
0	0	– (or 0)
1	24	24
2	44	20
3	56	12
4	60	4

A decrease in the amount of a good purchased would <u>decrease</u> total utility, and marginal utility will <u>increase</u>. As more of a product is purchased the marginal utility <u>decreases</u>.

b Look at the values in the marginal utility column above and state the law of economics they show.

<u>The law of diminishing marginal utility.</u>

c State the optimum purchase rule.

<u>P = MU</u>

d State the consumer equilibrium rule (or formula) a consumer should use to ensure they maximise total utility they receive from purchasing two products.

$$\frac{MUa}{price\ a} = \frac{MUb}{price\ b}$$

e The price of good A is $2 and the price of good B is $1.50. If a consumer evaluates the marginal utility of B to be 30 and he or she is in equilibrium with respect to purchases of A and B, then he or she must consider the marginal utility of A to be what?

$$\frac{MUa}{price\ a} = \frac{MUb}{price\ b} \qquad \frac{?}{2} = \frac{30}{1.50} \qquad MUa = 40$$

f Explain the significance of the law of diminishing marginal utility in deriving the individual demand curve.

<u>As consumption increases, MU decreases. The rational consumer attempting to maximise his/her satisfaction will be prepared to purchase to where P = MU. Consumers will only purchase additional units at a lower price. The individual demand curve is therefore derived from the individual MU curve.</u>

g Indicate if the following statements are correct or incorrect.

(i) The consumer gains the maximum utility for the money available when the quantity purchased is at a point where P > MU. <u>Incorrect</u>

(ii) The consumer gains the maximum utility for the money available when the quantity purchased is at a point where P = MU. <u>Correct</u>

(iii) When a consumer increases consumption of a good or service the MU tends to decrease and they will be prepared to pay less. <u>Correct</u>

(iv) The consumer's equilibrium occurs when the marginal utility per dollar of all goods and services is equal. <u>Correct</u>

ISBN 9780170241212
ISBN 9780170241229

3 Julian likes to hire videos or video games at the local store. Videos are $10 each and video games $8.
 a   Complete the table given.

Quantity of each product	Marginal utility of videos (utils)	MU per $ videos	Marginal utility of video games (utils)	MU per $ video games
1	80	8	56	7
2	40	4	40	5
3	20	2	32	4
4	10	1	24	3

 b   State the law of economics that the changing values of marginal utility show in the table.

The law of diminishing marginal utility.

 c   State the consumer equilibrium rule Julian needs to apply to maximise the total utility he receives from buying videos and video games.

$$\frac{MU\ videos}{price\ videos} = \frac{MU\ video\ games}{price\ video\ games}$$

 d   How many videos and video games should Julian purchase to maximise his total utility?

Number of videos 2

Number of video games 3

 e   Explain using the optimum purchase rule why Julian would buy fewer videos if their price increased.

The optimum purchase rule states P = MU, if the price of a video increases then price will exceed the

MU, and therefore the price paid for one more video would outweigh the satisfaction derived from it.

Julian would therefore purchase fewer videos, this will cause MU to rise (the law of diminishing

marginal utility) until it equals the new increased price.

ISBN 9780170241212
ISBN 9780170241229

REVIEW QUESTIONS

1 Alan is a Year 13 Economics student who likes drinking flavoured milk. Explain the concept of utility. In your answer you should:

- Complete the table below by calculating the missing values.
- Draw Alan's demand schedule for flavoured milk per day in the schedule provided.
- Define the law of diminishing marginal utility.
- Explain, using the law of diminishing marginal utility, why Alan's demand curve will slope downwards to the right. Refer to the table in your answer.

Alan's Utility Schedule for Flavoured Milk (per day)		
Number of bottles consumed	Total utility (cents)	Marginal utility (cents)
1	600	600
2	1 000	400
3	1 300	300
4	1 500	200
5	1 600	100

Alan's Demand Schedule for Flavoured Milk per day	
Price ($)	Quantity Demanded
1.00	5
2.00	4
3.00	3
4.00	2
6.00	1

The law of diminishing marginal utility states that as quantity consumed increases the extra satisfaction (MU) from consuming an extra unit decreases.

The price consumers are prepared to pay for a good depends on the marginal utility they receive from it (i.e., there is a relationship between price and marginal utility / consumer will continue to consume up to the point where P = MU).

Since MU falls as quantity increases (i.e., the law of diminishing MU) consumers will only buy larger quantities if the price falls to match their lower MU. A drop in price from $2 to $1 is required for Alan to buy an additional unit of flavoured milk.

So a demand curve must slope downward to the right with lower prices matching lower MUs of larger quantities consumed.

ISBN 9780170241212
ISBN 9780170241229

2   Mark Cambo enjoys hitting golf balls and often goes to the driving range to hit a basket of golf balls. He gives you the following information about his utility.

Explain the concept of utility. In your answer you should:

- Complete the table below by filling in the missing numbers.
- Plot Mark Cambo's demand curve for golf balls on the grid below.
- Name the law that explains why Mark gains less satisfaction with every basket of balls purchased.
- Use marginal utility to explain why Mark Cambo purchases more baskets of golf balls when the price of a basket of golf balls falls.

Mark Cambo's Utility Schedule for baskets of Golf Balls		
Quantity consumed (basket of balls)	Total utility (cents)	Marginal utility (cents)
1	600	600
2	1 000	400
3	1 200	200
4	1 250	50

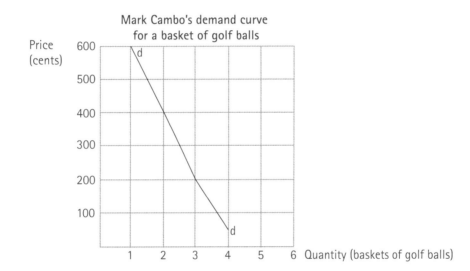

Mark Cambo's demand curve for a basket of golf balls

The law of diminishing marginal utility explains why Mark gains less satisfaction with every basket of golf balls purchased.

Mark will purchase a basket of golf balls until he reaches the point where P = MU (optimal purchase rule). When the price of a basket of golf balls falls, P < MU, there is an incentive for Mark to increase his consumption of baskets of golf balls. As he consumes additional units, MU will fall. Consequently, consumer equilibrium will be restored at a lower price and a corresponding lower marginal utility (P′ = MU′). A rational consumer (like Mark) will therefore increase the quantity he purchases when the price of a good falls.

PHOTOCOPYING PROHIBITED   ISBN 9780170241212
ISBN 9780170241229

3   A consumer, Jacob, assigns the following utility to successive levels of consumption.

Units consumed	Utility					
	Pizza	MU per $	Drink	MU per $	Wedges	MU per $
1	120	12	22	11	40	10
2	90	9	20	10	36	9
3	60	6	18	9	32	8
4	40	4	14	7	28	7
5	20	2	12	6	24	6
Price per unit	$10		$2		$4	

Help Jacob maximise the total utility he receives from purchasing pizza, drinks and wedges. In your answer you should:
- Complete the MU per $ column for each product in the table.
- State the consumer equilibrium rule (or formula) Jacob should use to ensure he maximises the total utility he receives.
- Assume Jacob has $20 to spend. What combination of goods will he buy?
- In what order will Jacob purchase pizza, drinks and wedges? Justify your answer for Jacob's fifth purchase.

$$\frac{\text{MU pizza}}{\text{price pizza}} = \frac{\text{MU drinks}}{\text{price drinks}} = \frac{\text{MU wedges}}{\text{price wedges}}$$

Jacob will purchase 1 pizza, 3 drinks and 1 lot of wedges.

Order of purchases	Price $	Total income spent
1st pizza	10	10
2nd drink	2	12
3rd= wedges	4	16
3rd= drink	2	18
5th drink	2	20

Jacob will buy a drink for his fifth purchase instead of another lot of wedges because at that stage he has only $2 left out of $20 income and therefore cannot afford to buy the wedges at a price of $4 or pizza at $10 each.

SELF-EVALUATION REVIEW
Tick (✔) which of the following you know the precise economic answers to (go back and learn those that you have not ticked).

	(✔) TICK
Explain the difference between total and marginal utility.	☐
Explain the law of diminishing utility.	☐
Intuitively derive how the individual demand curve is derived from the individual's marginal utility curve.	☐

ISBN 9780170241212
ISBN 9780170241229

Key concepts and terms: apply the law of diminishing returns to show its relationship to increasing costs (3.3).

DIMINISHING RETURNS

The **law of diminishing returns** refers to the idea that as more and more of a factor (input) is used, with at least one fixed factor, there is some point at which the increase in output will be at a decreasing rate.

In the table, we assume that workers are the only variable factor in the production process. The additions to output (marginal output) increase between the first and second workers. The additions to output reach a maximum on the second worker and thereafter the additional output falls as diminishing returns set in.

Number of workers	Total output	Marginal output
1	10	10
2	30	20
3	40	10
4	46	6
5	48	2
6	46	–2

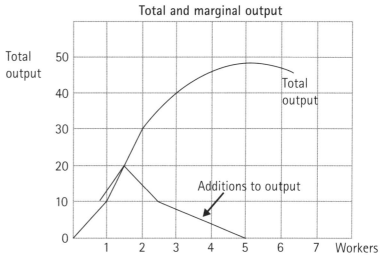

Firms will experience diminishing returns in the short run because, in the short run, at least one factor input is fixed. If additional quantities of other (variable) factors are added into the production process, the total output will increase at a diminishing rate (marginal product must eventually fall). This is because each factor has less of the fixed factor to work with, reducing its ability to produce (extra) output.

Diminishing returns will cause a firm's marginal costs to increase because as each additional variable unit produces less when diminishing returns are occurring, the production of extra units of output will require more and more of variable inputs to produce them (compared with earlier units). Therefore, it follows that the cost of each additional unit produced (i.e., MC) must increase because more inputs are being used to produce it. So, marginal cost must rise as output increases.

Increasing returns to a factor reflect that a firm's short-run average costs would be falling. The increased input of a factor results in increasing additions to output, or a decreased input results in a smaller decrease in output. If a firm decreases an input by 5% but output falls by only 4%, the addition to outputs is actually increasing. The production process must be more efficient than before and costs must be falling (in the short run).

Decreasing returns to a factor (or diminishing returns) reflect that the increase of one input results in decreasing additions to output. The firm increases an input by 5% but output rises by only 3%. Similarly a decrease in an input would result in a larger decrease in output. An input falls by 10% and output decreases by 12%. Both these examples show that the production process has become inefficient. The short-run average costs (**SAC**) will eventually rise.

RETURNS TO SCALE (OR FACTORS)

In the long run firms can change all inputs and the firm can be more adaptable and change the size of its operations.

With the increase in size of the firm's operations if the average cost per unit falls, this is known as **economies of scale** or **increasing returns to factors**. An increase in inputs will result in a more than proportionate increase in output.

A firm increases its inputs (the 's' reflects all factors rather than a single input is changed, as is the case in the short run) by 10% and output increases by more than 10%. The firm's long-run average costs (LRAC) must be falling and the production process is efficient.

Economies of scale or increasing returns to factors may be due to existing or new machinery being more efficiently utilised. Also, as output increases, fixed costs are spread over a greater number of units of output. As these average fixed costs fall they will tend to pull down long-run average costs. A firm that is buying in bulk is possibly able to negotiate preferential terms (discounts), and financial economies are possible because large firms may receive lower rates of interest on funds borrowed.

Diseconomies of scale or decreasing returns to factors are possible. The increase in the size of the firm's operation may see cost per unit rise as the inputs combinations used in the production process become less and less efficient. These diseconomies would be illustrated with the long-run average costs rising. An increase in inputs results in a smaller increase in output, for example inputs increase by 10% and output increases by 8%. Similarly if a decrease in inputs results in a larger decrease in output, this reflects that the production process is less efficient and costs per unit are increasing. As inputs decrease by 20% the output decreases by more than 20%.

Graph showing the firm's long-run average costs

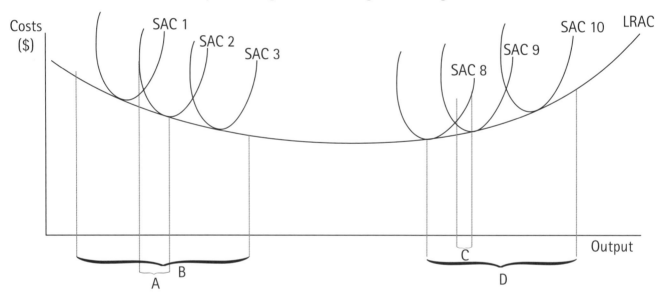

Position	Description
A	SAC falling, increasing returns to a factor
B	LRAC falling, economies of scale
C	SAC rising, diminishing returns
D	LRAC rising, diseconomies of scale

ISBN 9780170241212
ISBN 9780170241229

KEY TERMS AND IDEAS

Diminishing returns	Occurs in the short-run when there is at least one fixed input; the additions to output at some stage start to decrease.
Why firms experience diminishing returns in the short run	In the short-run, at least one factor input is fixed. If additional quantities of other (variable) factors are added into the production process, the total output will increase at a diminishing rate (marginal product must eventually fall). This is because each factor has less of the fixed factor to work with, reducing its ability to produce (extra) output.
Why diminishing returns cause a firm's marginal costs to increase	As each additional variable unit produces less when diminishing returns are occurring, the production of extra units of output will require more and more of variable inputs to produce them (compared with earlier units). Therefore, it follows that the cost of each additional unit produced (i.e., MC) must increase because more inputs are being used to produce it. So, marginal cost must rise as output increases.
Increasing returns to a factor	A firm's short-run average costs are falling (efficient output-to-input change). This means that an increase in input causes a larger increase in output; or that a decrease in input causes a smaller decrease in output.
Diminishing returns or decreasing returns to a factor	A firm's short-run average costs are rising (inefficient input-to-output change). This means that an increase in input causes a smaller increase in output; or that a decrease in input causes a larger decrease in output.
Economies of scale or increasing returns to factors (scale)	Is when a firm's long-run average cost curve is falling (efficient change of inputs to outputs). This means that an increase in inputs causes a more than proportionate increase in output; or that a decrease in inputs causes a less than proportionate decrease in output.
Diseconomies of scale or decreasing returns to factors (scale)	Is when a firm's long-run average cost curve is rising (inefficient change of inputs to output). This means that a decrease in inputs causes a more than proportionate decrease in output; or that an increase in inputs causes a less than proportionate increase in output.

STUDENT NOTES: DIMINISHING RETURNS

Diminishing returns will occur in the short run when there is at least one fixed input; the additions to output at some stage start to decrease.

Firms experience diminishing returns in the short run because in the short run, at least one factor input is fixed. If additional quantities of other (variable) factors are added into the production process, the total output will increase at a diminishing rate (marginal product must eventually fall).

This is because each factor has less of the fixed factor to work with, reducing its ability to produce (extra) output.

Diminishing returns cause a firm's marginal costs to increase because as each additional variable unit produces less when diminishing returns are occurring, the production of extra units of output will require more and more variable inputs to produce them (compared with earlier units). Therefore, it follows that the cost of each additional unit produced (i.e., MC) must increase because more inputs are being used to produce it. So, marginal cost must rise as output increases. A firm will only supply a product if it covers the marginal costs of producing it. As MC increase as output increases, firms will require a higher price to increase the quantity supplied of a product.

Increasing returns to a factor mean that a firm's short-run average costs are falling (efficient output-to-input change). This means that an increase in input causes a larger increase in output; or that a decrease in input causes a smaller decrease in output. Initially, increasing returns to a factor cause MC to fall.

ISBN 9780170241212
ISBN 9780170241229

PRACTISE QUESTIONS AND TASKS

1 a Explain why firms experience diminishing returns in the short run.

In the short run, at least one factor input is fixed. If additional quantities of other (variable) factors are added into the production process, the total output will increase at a diminishing rate (marginal product must eventually fall). This is because each factor has less of the fixed factor to work with, reducing its ability to produce (extra) output.

b Explain why diminishing returns cause a firm's marginal costs to increase.

Since each additional variable unit produces less when diminishing returns are occurring, the production of extra units of output will require more and more of variable inputs to produce them (compared with earlier units). Therefore, it follows that the cost of each additional unit produced (i.e., MC) must increase because more inputs are being used to produce it. So, marginal cost must rise as output increases.

c For each table indicate when diminishing returns sets in (i) after the ... (ii) with the ....

Output	10	100	250	450	550
Machines	1	2	3	4	5

(i) after the <u>fourth machine</u>   (ii) with the <u>fifth machine</u>

Workers	1	2	3	4	5
Total output	5	15	40	90	120

(i) after the <u>fourth worker</u>   (ii) with the <u>fifth worker</u>

Output	20	50	90	150	250	260	265
Workers	1	2	3	4	5	6	7

(i) after the <u>fifth worker</u>   (ii) with the <u>sixth worker</u>

Machine	Output
1	50
2	150
3	160
4	165
5	167

(i) after the <u>second machine</u>   (ii) with the <u>third machine</u>

2 **a** Why does the marginal cost curve initially fall and then rise?

Initially increasing returns and the more efficient use of resources leads to falling MC but eventually, in the short run, diminishing returns will occur causing MC to increase.

b Explain why firms experience diminishing returns in the short run.

In the short run, at least one factor input is fixed. If additional quantities of other (variable) factors are added into the production process, the total output will increase at a diminishing rate (marginal product must eventually fall). This is because each factor has less of the fixed factor to work with, reducing its ability to produce (extra) output.

c Explain why diminishing returns cause a firm's marginal costs to increase.

Since each additional variable unit produces less when diminishing returns are occurring, the production of extra units of output will require more and more of variable inputs to produce them (compared with earlier units). Therefore, it follows that the cost of each additional unit produced (i.e., MC) must increase because more inputs are being used to produce it. So, marginal cost must rise as output increases.

d **(i)** Complete the table below by calculating the missing numbers. **Note:** Factory workers are paid $10 per hour.

Table 2: Productivity of Workers at a Golf Club Set Producing Firm			
Total Output (Number of golf club sets)	Total hours worked	Hours required to increase output by one unit	Marginal cost of producing extra units
1	10	10	$100
2	15	5	$50
3	40	25	$250
4	70	30	$300
5	110	40	$400

(ii) At which output level in the table do diminishing returns start? 3

(iii) Explain why diminishing returns cause the marginal cost of golf club sets production to rise.

If diminishing returns are occurring, more variable factors are required to produce an extra unit of output, so it will cost more to produce. In Table 2, it takes five extra hours of labour to produce the second golf set, so it costs $50. But diminishing returns start with the production of the third golf set, and it takes 20 more hours to produce (i.e., 25 hours), so its marginal cost is higher – costing $250 to produce.

ISBN 9780170241212
ISBN 9780170241229

REVIEW QUESTIONS

Output	200	300	400	500	600
Marginal costs	30	25	60	78	100

1 Explain the relationship between ouput and marginal costs. In your answer you should:

- Draw a sketch diagram of a marginal cost curve and explain its shape.
- Explain why diminishing returns cause a firm's marginal costs to increase.
- Describe the relationship between marginal cost and the quantity supplied of a product by a firm.

The marginal cost curve will initially fall and then rise because initially increasing returns to a factor and the more efficient use of resources leads to falling MC but in the short run eventually diminishing returns will occur causing MC to increase.

MC

Because each additional variable unit produces less when diminishing returns are occurring, the production of extra units of output will require more and more variable inputs to produce them (compared with earlier units). Therefore, it follows that the cost of each additional unit produced (i.e., MC) must increase because more inputs are being used to produce it. So, marginal cost must rise as output increases.

A firm will only supply a product if it covers the marginal costs of producing it. Because MC increase as output increases firms will require a higher price to increase the quantity supplied of a product.

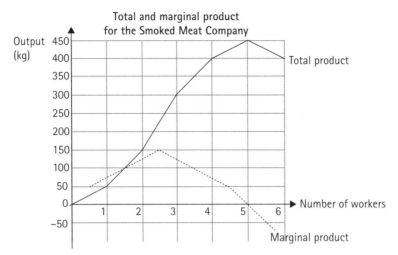

2 Explain the relationship between diminishing returns and a firm's marginal costs. In your answer you should

- State when diminishing returns set in.
- Explain why firms experience diminishing returns in the short run.
- Explain why diminishing returns cause a firm's marginal costs to increase.

Diminishing returns set in after the employment of the third worker

In the short run, at least one factor input is fixed. If additional quantities of other (variable) factors are added into the production process, the total output will increase at a diminishing rate (marginal product must eventually fall). This is because each factor has less of the fixed factor to work with, reducing its ability to produce (extra) output.

Because each additional variable unit produces less when diminishing returns are occurring, the production of extra units of output will require more and more variable inputs to produce them (compared with earlier units). Therefore, it follows that the cost of each additional unit produced (i.e., MC) must increase because more inputs are being used to produce it. So, marginal cost must rise as output increases.

SELF-EVALUATION REVIEW

Tick (✔) which of the following you know the precise economic answers to (go back and learn those that you have not ticked).

	(✔) TICK
Can define diminishing returns.	☐
Can identify when diminishing returns set in.	☐
Can distinguish between increasing returns to a factor, economies of scale, diminishing returns and diseconomies of scale	☐

ISBN 9780170241212
ISBN 9780170241229

3 BREAK–EVEN AND SHUTDOWN

Key concepts and terms: shutdown, break-even, the shape of the marginal cost curve and supply for the perfect competitor (3.3).

BREAK-EVEN AND SHUTDOWN POINTS FOR A FIRM

Break-even is the price at which revenue covers all economic costs. On the graph the value of break-even is shown as the value of Pb. The value of break-even position is at the price $7. The two cost curves equal to the price at the breakeven point are MC and AC.

Shutdown is the price where revenue just covers variable costs. The firm will cease operations and use no variable inputs. Fixed costs will still have to be paid but from some other source. Shutdown is shown as the value Ps on the graph. The shutdown point is at a level where price is just equal to average variable costs (AVC). At this point the firm is indifferent to whether it continues to produce or shuts down. The value of shutdown position is at the price $5. The two cost curves equal to the price at the shutdown point are MC and AVC.

Between the shutdown and break-even points (that is, between Pb and Ps), the firm covers all its variable costs and some of the revenue it makes contributes towards its fixed costs. The firm will continue operating because if it shuts down it will still have to pay all its fixed costs.

At any revenue (or price) below shutdown, the firm fails to cover all its variable costs and will save these costs by not producing.

Break–even and shutdown points

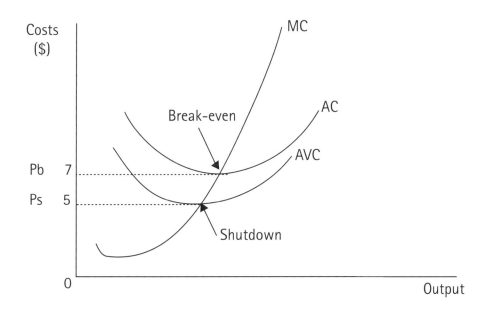

ISBN 9780170241212
ISBN 9780170241229

Deriving the supply curve from the marginal cost curve

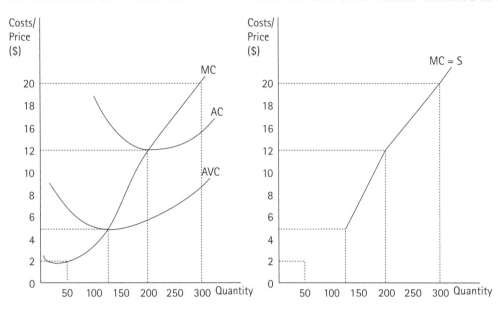

Supply schedule from the MC curve	
Price ($)	Quantity Supplied
2	0
5	125
12	200
20	300

A firm's supply curve is drawn as *that part of MC above AVC (or shutdown)*.

At $2 quantity supplied is zero (0) because the supply curve is derived from MC above AVC (or shutdown). The firm's supply curve is derived from the MC curve and it starts from the minimum of the AVC.

Since a firm's supply curve is the MC curve, it will shift to the right if costs decrease or shift to the left if costs increase.

Key terms and ideas

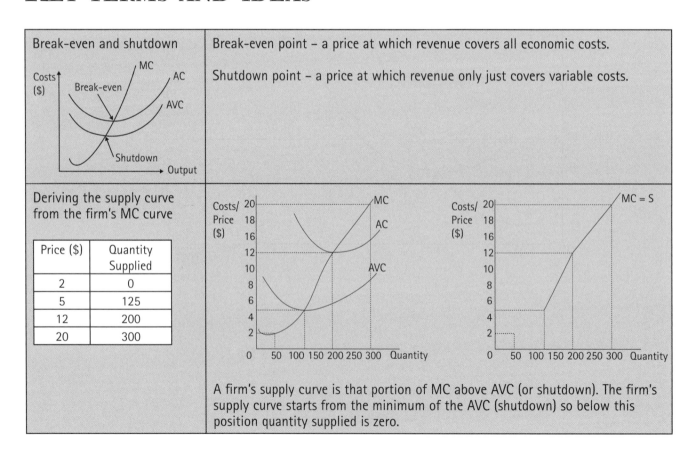

Break-even and shutdown	Break-even point – a price at which revenue covers all economic costs. Shutdown point – a price at which revenue only just covers variable costs.
Deriving the supply curve from the firm's MC curve	

Price ($)	Quantity Supplied
2	0
5	125
12	200
20	300

A firm's supply curve is that portion of MC above AVC (or shutdown). The firm's supply curve starts from the minimum of the AVC (shutdown) so below this position quantity supplied is zero.

ISBN 9780170241212
ISBN 9780170241229

STUDENT NOTES: BREAK-EVEN AND SHUTDOWN

Break-even point is at a price at which revenue covers all economic costs. The two cost curves equal to the price at the break-even point are MC and AC.

Shutdown point is at a price at which revenue only just covers variable costs. The two cost curves equal to the price at the shutdown point are MC and AVC.

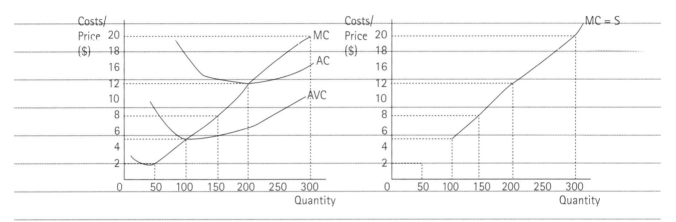

A firm's supply curve is that part of MC above AVC (or shutdown). The firm's supply curve starts from the minimum of the AVC (shutdown) so below this position quantity supplied is zero.

Supply schedule for a firm using MC curve	
Price ($)	Quantity supplied
2	0
8	150
12	200
20	300

PRACTISE QUESTIONS AND TASKS

1 Use the diagram to answer the questions below.

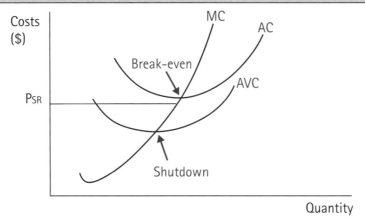

a Label the curves and identify and label the break-even and shutdown points.

b (i) What is the vertical distance between AC and AVC equal to? <u>AFC</u>

(ii) Is this gap a constant? <u>No</u>

c (i) When the firm is not producing it must still pay what types of costs? <u>FC</u>

(ii) What costs are directly related to production? <u>VC</u>

(iii) If the firm is not producing, what is the value of these costs? <u>zero</u>

d Write *fixed costs* or *variable costs* for the following terms.

Rent	<u>fixed</u>	Wages	<u>variable</u>
Raw materials	<u>variable</u>	Debt servicing	<u>fixed</u>
Interest	<u>fixed</u>		

e What is debt servicing?

<u>Interest payments and repayments of principal on loans.</u>

f Define the following terms.

Break-even: <u>A price at which revenue covers all economic costs.</u>

Shutdown: <u>A price at which revenue only just covers variable costs.</u>

g Complete this statement.

If a firm ceases its operation it must still pay <u>fixed</u> costs. If market price is above the level of average variable cost, it can cover its <u>variable</u> costs and still have something left over to pay its fixed costs, it may as well <u>continue</u> operating. If price falls below AVC, there is nothing left over to contribute to <u>fixed</u> costs and variable costs are not fully covered, then the firm should <u>shut down</u>.

ISBN 9780170241212
ISBN 9780170241229

2 a Write if the following statements are *correct* or *incorrect*.

   (i)   A firm's supply curve is equal to its AC curve.   incorrect

   (ii)   A firm's supply curve is equal to its MC curve above AVC.   correct

   (iii) When revenue covers all economic costs it is at shutdown.   incorrect

   (iv)   Break-even is when revenue covers variable costs only.   incorrect

   (v)   At any revenue below shutdown, the firm will save paying variable costs

          by not operating but will still have to pay fixed costs.   correct

   (vi)   Break-even is when revenue covers all economic costs.   correct

b Label the curves on the diagram and clearly label the break-even point (label B) and the shutdown point (label SD).

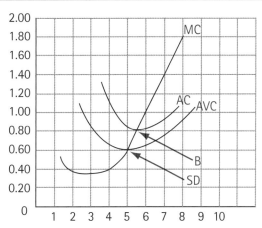

Costs/Price/Revenue ($)

c Give the value of: (i) Shutdown $0.60   (ii) Break-even $0.80   .

d What cost concept is represented by the vertical gap between AVC and AC?   AFC

e Why does this gap narrow as output rises?

AFC declines with increasing output because the FC are spread over a greater number of units of output.

Therefore because ATC = AFC + AVC, a higher proportion of TC will be made up of VC as output rises so

the gap narrows.

f Which two cost curves are equal to the price at:

(i) shutdown point? MC and AVC   (ii) break-even point? MC and AC   .

g Explain why the firm can continue producing in the short run at $0.70.

Firm has a price which covers AVC and makes some contribution towards FC.

REVIEW QUESTIONS

1 A firm's supply curve is the same as its marginal cost curve.

Discuss the relationship between marginal cost and a firm's supply. In your answer you should:

- Define individual supply and marginal cost.
- Explain how marginal cost affects the quantity a producer is willing to supply.
- Explain any difference that exists between the supply curve and the marginal cost curve of a firm.

Supply is the amount of a good/service producer's offer for sale at each price (ceteris paribus).

Marginal cost is the addition to total cost resulting from the production of an extra unit of output.

A firm will only offer a good/service for sale if the price they receive covers the cost of producing it (i.e.,the MC).

Supply = MC curve above the shutdown point, i.e., MC above P = minimum AVC in short run because there is no point in producing if revenue earned not sufficient to even cover additional costs of resources needed to produce output, or MC above P = minimum AVC in short run because losses will be reduced if shut down (stop producing) and only have to pay fixed costs, or MC above P = minimum AC in long run because there is no point in producing if earning sub-normal profit so the owner would be better off shifting their resources to their next best alternative.

ISBN 9780170241212
ISBN 9780170241229

2   The average variable cost curve is important in determining the short-run supply curve for the perfectly competitive producer.

Explain the relationship between a firm's average variable cost curve and its supply curve. In your answer you should:

- Label the curves in Graph one and complete the supply schedule next to it.
- Label the shutdown point (label S) and break-even point (label B) on Graph one.
- Define the terms break-even and shutdown and indicate which two cost curves are equal to the price at each point.
- Explain how a firm's supply curve is derived from MC.

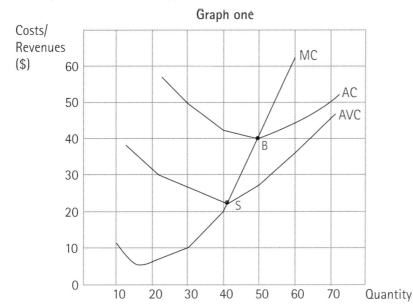

Graph one

Supply schedule	
Price ($)	Quantity
10	0
20	0
30	45
40	50
50	55
60	58

Break-even is a price at which revenue covers all economic costs. The two cost curves equal to the price at the break-even point are MC and AC.

Shutdown is a price at which revenue only just covers variable costs. The two cost curves equal to the price at the shutdown point are MC and AVC.

The short-run supply curve for the perfect competitor is the MC curve above the minimum AVC curve.

At any price less than the minimum of the AVC curve the firm will shut down in the short run.

SELF-EVALUATION REVIEW

Tick (✔) which of the following you know the precise economic answers to (go back and learn those that you have not ticked).

	(✔) TICK
Identify the shutdown and break-even points.	☐
Define shutdown and break-even.	☐

4   PRICE ELASTICITY OF DEMAND, Eₚ

Key concepts and terms: price elasticity of demand, calculation of price elasticity of demand, reasons for differing elasticities, significance for firms in their pricing decisions (3.3).

PRICE ELASTICITY OF DEMAND

Price elasticity of demand (Ep) measures the *responsiveness of quantity demanded of a good or service to changes in its price.*

To calculate price elasticity of demand we divide the percentage change in quantity demanded by the percentage change in price.

Percentage change method

$$Ep = \frac{\%\Delta QD}{\%\Delta P}$$ where

Ep	=	coefficient of price elasticity of demand
%ΔQD	=	percentage change in quantity demanded
%ΔP	=	percentage change in price

Note the final number (coefficient) will always be a negative number because price and quantity demanded always occur in opposite directions. To be strictly accurate the coefficient should be written as a negative number. However, it is common practice in economics to ignore the negative sign.

When Ep > 1 the price elasticity of demand is termed elastic.
When Ep = 1 the price elasticity of demand is termed unitary.
When Ep < 1 the price elasticity of demand is termed inelastic.

For example: As the price of the product fell by 20% the quantity demanded rose 25%.

$$Ep = \frac{\%\Delta QD}{\%\Delta P} = \frac{25\%}{-20\%} = -1.25 = 1.25 \text{ elastic}$$

Price elasticity of demand can also be calculated by using the midpoint method. The midpoint method is explained below.

Midpoint method

$$Ep = \frac{\left(\dfrac{\text{change in quantity demanded}}{\text{midpoint of quantity demanded}} \right)}{\left(\dfrac{\text{change in price}}{\text{midpoint of the prices indicated}} \right)} = \frac{\left(\dfrac{\dfrac{\Delta Q}{Q1 + Q2}}{2} \right)}{\left(\dfrac{\dfrac{\Delta P}{P1 + P2}}{2} \right)}$$

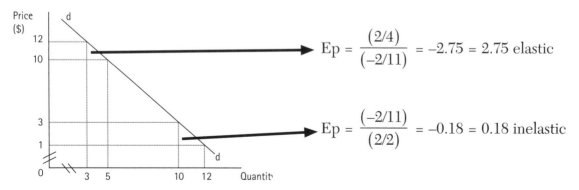

$$Ep = \frac{(2/4)}{(-2/11)} = -2.75 = 2.75 \text{ elastic}$$

$$Ep = \frac{(-2/11)}{(2/2)} = -0.18 = 0.18 \text{ inelastic}$$

Price elasticity of demand is a point concept so a single demand curve can have a range of elasticities, typically relatively elastic at the top end and relatively inelastic at the lower end.

ISBN 9780170241212
ISBN 9780170241229

In extreme cases, slope does indicate elasticity.

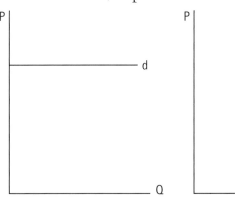

Perfectly (or infinitely) elastic –
a horizontal curve, Ep = ∞

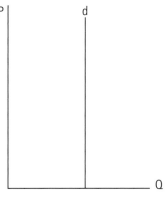

Perfectly inelastic (zero elasticity)
– a vertical curve, Ep = 0

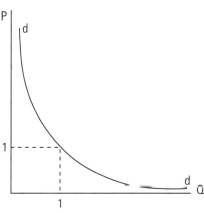

Unit elasticity – rectangular hyperbola,
Ep = 1

Price elasticity of demand can also be calculated using the revenue method, which compares the change in **price (P)** with the change in **total revenue (TR)**. Total revenue (TR) equals **price (P)** times **quantity (Q)**. The table gives a summary of elasticity using the revenue method.

Price and total revenue relationship		Elasticity
P ⬍; TR remains unchanged	Any change in price will see total revenue remain the same	Unitary
P ↑; TR ↑ or P ↓; TR ↓	Price and total revenue changes are in the same direction	Inelastic
P ↑; TR ↓ or P ↓; TR ↑	Price and total revenue changes are in the opposite direction	Elastic

For example
Unitary elasticity (Ep = 1)
Any change in price results in no change in total revenue.

Price (P) $	Quantity demanded (Q)	Total revenue (TR) $
25	4	100
20	5	100

Inelastic demand (Ep < 1)
When price increases so will total revenue and if price decreases so will total revenue. Changes in price and total revenue move in the same direction. In the example shown, as price increases from 60 cents to 80 cents, total revenue increases from $6.00 to $7.20, so Ep is inelastic.

Price (P) $	Quantity demanded (Q)	Total revenue (TR) $
60c	10	$6.00
80c	9	$7.20

Elastic demand (Ep > 1)
When price increases total revenue will decrease or if price decreases then total revenue will increase. When the changes in price and total revenue are in opposite directions, so Ep is elastic. As price decreases from $12 to $10 the total revenue increases from $1,200 to $1,300.

Price (P) $	Quantity demanded (Q)	Total revenue (TR) $
$12	100	$1 200
$10	130	$1 300

FACTORS THAT DETERMINE ELASTICITY OF DEMAND

Inelastic demand includes products that tend to have no or few close substitutes and are often considered necessities such as bread, milk, medical services. The products may be addictive such as cigarettes or alcohol. When the relative cost of the commodity is a small fraction of total outlay then the demand will be inelastic, for example a newspaper.

Products that have **elastic demand** have many substitutes and are often considered luxuries such as fashion clothing and cars because there are substitutes such as walking, catching a bus, etc.

APPLICATION OF ELASTICITY

When price elasticity of demand is less than one, this means that a given change in price causes a less than proportionate change in quantity demanded and indicates inelastic demand.

When price elasticity of demand is greater than one, this means that a given change in price causes a more than proportionate change in quantity demanded and indicates elastic demand.

If a firm desires to increase revenue it would increase price if the product was inelastic in nature and decrease price if the product was elastic in nature.

Government will raise more revenue from taxes on products that are inelastic in nature such as cigarettes and beer.

The incidence of a tax will fall more heavily on the consumer if demand is inelastic and more on the producer when demand is elastic. The incidence of the tax refers to who actually pays the tax.

KEY TERMS AND IDEAS

Price elasticity of demand (Ep)	Measures the responsiveness of quantity demanded of a good or service to changes in its price
Formula to calculate price elasticity of demand midpoint method (Ep > 1 is elastic Ep = 1 is unitary Ep < 1 is inelastic)	$Ep = \dfrac{\left(\dfrac{\text{change in quantity demanded}}{\text{midpoint of quantity demanded}}\right)}{\left(\dfrac{\text{change in price}}{\text{midpoint of the prices indicated}}\right)} = \dfrac{\left(\dfrac{\Delta Q}{\dfrac{Q1 + Q2}{2}}\right)}{\left(\dfrac{\Delta P}{\dfrac{P1 + P2}{2}}\right)}$
Price elasticity of demand using the revenue method	TR remains unchanged when the price changes, Ep = 1 TR and price changes occur in the same direction, e.g., P↓ TR↓, Ep < 1 TR and price changes occur in opposite directions, e.g., P↑ TR↓, Ep > 1
Inelastic demand	A given change in price causes a less than proportionate change in quantity demanded.
Elastic demand	A given change in price causes a more than proportionate change in quantity demanded.
Features of goods and services that are inelastic in nature	Addictive, few substitutes, often considered necessities, e.g., food, cigarettes. The incidence of a sales tax falls more on the consumer. Takes a small proportion of total income spent.
Features of goods and services that are elastic in nature	Many substitutes, often considered luxuries, e.g. cars, meals out. Incidence of a tax will fall more on the producer. Takes a high proportion of total income spent.

ISBN 9780170241212
ISBN 9780170241229

STUDENT NOTES: PRICE ELASTICITY OF DEMAND

Price elasticity of demand (Ep) – measures the responsiveness of quantity demanded of a good (or service) to changes in its price.

Goods (or services) that are elastic in nature (Ep > 1) – often considered luxuries, many substitutes, takes a high percentage of income spent, e.g., new cars, houses. A given change in price evokes a more than proportionate change in quantity demanded.

Goods (or services) that are inelastic in nature (Ep < 1) – necessities, few (if any) substitutes, takes a small percentage of income spent, can be addictive in nature, e.g., cigarettes, alcohol, bread, milk. A given change in price evokes a less than proportionate change in quantity demanded.

Revenue method for Ep – Ep = 1 (unitary) P $\updownarrow$ TR unchanged

Ep > 1 (elastic) P $\uparrow$ TR $\downarrow$

Ep < 1 (inelastic) P $\uparrow$ TR $\downarrow$

Relatively inelastic demand curve   Relatively elastic demand curve

PRACTISE QUESTIONS AND TASKS

1 a Define price elasticity of demand and give the formula to calculate Ep.

Ep measures the responsiveness of quantity demanded of a good or service to changes in its price.

$$Ep = \frac{\dfrac{\Delta QD}{midpt\ QD}}{\dfrac{\Delta P}{midpt\ price}} \qquad or \qquad Ep = \frac{\%\Delta QD}{\%\Delta P}$$

b Work out price elasticity of demand for each question below. Show your working (round to two decimal places). Use the midpoint method.

(i) The price of coffee rose from $15 per kg to $20 per kg and sales fell from 100 kg to 80 kg per week.

$$Ep = \frac{\left(\dfrac{-20}{90}\right)}{\left(\dfrac{5}{17.5}\right)} = -0.777 = 0.78 \quad inelastic$$

(ii)

Price ($)	Quantity demanded
1.50	100
1.70	95

$$Ep = \frac{\left(\dfrac{-5}{97.5}\right)}{\left(\dfrac{.20}{1.60}\right)} = -0.410 = 0.41 \ inelastic$$

(iii) Work out the Ep on the curve at the positions indicated.

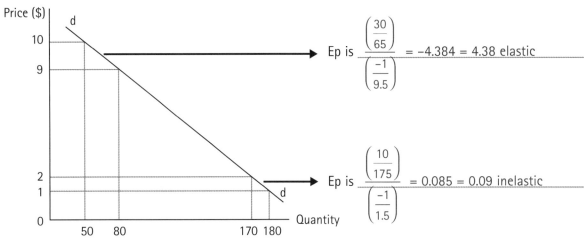

$$Ep\ is\ \frac{\left(\dfrac{30}{65}\right)}{\left(\dfrac{-1}{9.5}\right)} = -4.384 = 4.38\ elastic$$

$$Ep\ is\ \frac{\left(\dfrac{10}{175}\right)}{\left(\dfrac{-1}{1.5}\right)} = 0.085 = 0.09\ inelastic$$

c Complete the table by giving possible explanations for the price elasticity of demand coefficient indicated.

Product (and price elasticity of demand coefficient)	Possible explanations
Toilet paper (0.23)	Toilet paper is a necessity. There are no substitutes for toilet paper. Takes a small proportion of total income spent.
New car (2.45)	A new car is a luxury. There are many substitutes. Takes a high proportion of total income spent.

ISBN 9780170241212
ISBN 9780170241229

2 Calculate price elasticity of demand for each of the following questions (to two decimal places). Work out Ep using (i) the midpoint method and (ii) the percentage change method. Show your working.

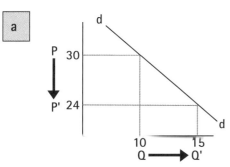

a

(i) $Ep = \dfrac{\left(\dfrac{5}{12.5}\right)}{\left(\dfrac{-6}{27}\right)} = -1.80 = 1.80$ elastic

(ii) $Ep = \dfrac{(50\%)}{(-20\%)} = -2.50 = 2.50$ elastic

b

	Price $	Quantity demanded
Old situation	25	100
New situation	30	60

(i) $Ep = \dfrac{\left(\dfrac{-40}{80}\right)}{\left(\dfrac{5}{27.5}\right)} = -2.75 = 2.75$ elastic

(ii) $Ep = \dfrac{(-40\%)}{(20\%)} = -2.00 = 2.00$ elastic

c Complete the table.

	Relative changes in price/revenue	Elasticity – unitary, inelastic, elastic
(i)	Price increases and total revenue remains unchanged	unitary
(ii)	Price increases and total revenue increases	inelastic
(iii)	Total revenue increases when price rises from $10 to $12	inelastic
(iv)	P↓ TR↓	inelastic
(v)	P↓ TR remains the same	unitary
(vi)	Price decreases and total revenue increases	elastic
(vii)	TR↑ when price falls	elastic
(viii)	Revenue remains the same when price falls	unitary
(ix)	Change in price and total revenue are in the same direction	inelastic
(x)	TR↑ P↑ or P↓ TR↓	inelastic
(xi)	Changes in TR and P go in the opposite direction	elastic

d (i) Give reasons why the price elasticity of demand coefficient of wiper blades is 0.19.

A small percentage of income is spent on wiper blades. There are few, if any, substitutes for wiper blades. Wiper blades are a necessity.

(ii) Indicate what will happen to a firm's revenue if they increase the price. Explain why.

Total revenue will increase because the given change in price will cause a less than proportionate change in quantity demanded.

PHOTOCOPYING PROHIBITED   ISBN 9780170241212
ISBN 9780170241229

3 Indicate the price elasticity of demand indicated by the situation outlined in the table below.

	Situation	Elasticity of demand
a	The response to a given change in price is an exactly proportionate change in quantity demanded	Unitary
b	The response to a given change in price is a more than proportionate change in quantity demanded	Elastic demand
c	The response to a given change in price is a less than proportionate change in quantity demanded	Inelastic demand
d	A given change in prices evokes a more than proportionate change in quantity demanded	Elastic demand
e	$\%\Delta$ price $<$ $\%\Delta$ quantity demanded	Elastic demand
f	$\%\Delta$ price $=$ $\%\Delta$ quantity demanded	Unitary
g	$\%\Delta$ QD $<$ $\%\Delta$ price	Inelastic demand

4 Doctor visits fell from 10 000 to 9 000 when price increased from $25 to $30. What is the price elasticity of demand for doctor visits? Give a possible reason for doctor visits, relating it to the Ep you calculated.

$$Ep = \frac{\left(\dfrac{-1000}{9\,500}\right)}{\left(\dfrac{5}{27.5}\right)} = -0.578 = 0.58$$

Inelastic. Doctors are a necessity/few substitutes if you are sick.

5 The brewery decides to increase the price of a jug from $4.50 to $5.00 and the quantity sold decreases from 7 500 to 7 300.

    a   Work out the change in revenue from the price increase. Was this an increase or decrease in revenue?

P	Q	TR		
$4.50	7 500	$33 750	P ↑ TR ↑	
$5.00	7 300	$36 500	revenue increased by $2 750	

    b   Work out Ep using the midpoint method.

$$Ep = \frac{\left(\dfrac{-200}{7\,400}\right)}{\left(\dfrac{0.50}{4.75}\right)} = -0.256 = 0.26 \text{ inelastic}$$

6 a   A car firm sells new cars for $25 000 and sells 10 000. What is the revenue made?

    $250 million ($25 000 x 10 000)

    b   When the price is slashed to $20 000 they sell 13 000. What is the revenue made?

    $260 million ($20 000 x 13 000)

    c   From this information what is Ep, and at what price would you sell cars for and why?

    Ep = elastic.   PR ↓   TR ↑   if you want to increase revenue sell at $20 000

ISBN 9780170241212
ISBN 9780170241229

REVIEW QUESTIONS

1 Price elasticity of demand is a point concept.

Explain price elasticity of demand using the graph below. In your answer you should:

- Define 'price elasticity of demand'.
- Calculate price elasticity of demand along the demand curve. Use the midpoint method and show your working.
- Describe the features of products that are elastic or inelastic in nature.

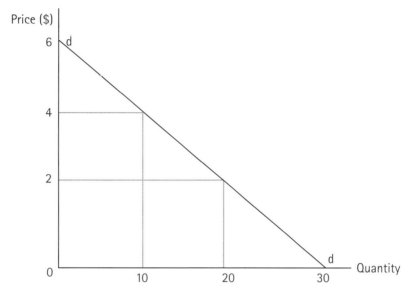

Ep between $6 and $4: $Ep = \dfrac{\left(\dfrac{-10}{5}\right)}{\left(\dfrac{2}{5}\right)} = -5 = 5$ elastic

Ep between $4 and $2: $Ep = \dfrac{\left(\dfrac{-10}{15}\right)}{\left(\dfrac{2}{3}\right)} = -1 = 1$ unitary

Ep between $2 and $0: $Ep = \dfrac{\left(\dfrac{-10}{25}\right)}{\left(\dfrac{2}{1}\right)} = -0.2 = 0.2$ inelastic

Price elasticity of demand measures the responsiveness of quantity demanded of a good or service to changes in its price.

The calculations above show that a demand curve can have a range of elasticity, typically elastic at the top end of a demand curve and inelastic at the bottom end.

Features of goods and services that are inelastic in nature are that they may be addictive, few substitutes, often considered necessities, e.g., food, cigarettes. Take a small proportion of total income spent.

Features of goods and services that are elastic in nature are that they have many substitutes, often considered luxuries, e.g. cars, meals out. Take a high proportion of total income spent.

ISBN 9780170241212
ISBN 9780170241229

2 Various factors determine the price elasticity of demand for a product. The demand coefficient of water is 0.15, coffee 0.56 and meals out at a restaurant 1.35. Firms use this knowledge in their pricing decisions. Explain factors that determine price elasticity of demand and how firms use this knowledge. In your answer you should:

- Explain factors that influence price elasticity of demand with reference to the information above.
- Explain how firms will use a knowledge of price elasticity of demand in their pricing decisions.

Factors that determine a product's elasticity include if it is a necessity or a luxury, the availability of substitutes and proportion of total income spent. Inelastic demand includes products that tend to have no or few close substitutes and are often considered necessities such as bread, milk, medical services. The products may be addictive such as cigarettes or alcohol. When the relative cost of the commodity is a small fraction of total outlay then the demand will be inelastic, for example a newspaper. Elastic demands include products that have many substitutes and are often considered luxuries such as fashion clothing and cars as there are substitutes such as walking, catching a bus, etc.

Water is inelastic in nature because water is a necessity. There are no substitutes for water and it takes a small proportion of total income spent.

Coffee is inelastic in nature because coffee is addictive/necessity. There are few or no substitutes for coffee and it takes a small proportion of total income spent.

Meals out at a restaurant are elastic in nature because they are a luxury. There are many substitutes. Can take a high proportion of total income spent.

Firms are aware that when price elasticity of demand is inelastic that a given change in price causes a less than proportionate change in quantity demanded and if a product is elastic in nature this means that a given change in price causes a more than proportionate change in quantity demanded. Therefore if a firm desires to increase revenue it would increase price if the product was inelastic in nature and decrease price if the product was elastic in nature.

ISBN 9780170241212
ISBN 9780170241229

3 The price elasticity of demand coefficient of overseas trips is 2.67.
Fully explain the price elasticity of demand for overseas trips. In your answer you should:

- Define price elasticity of demand.
- Explain why the price elasticity of demand for overseas trips is elastic.
- Explain what will happen to the total revenue for producers of overseas trip if the price falls by 4%.

Price elasticity of demand measures the responsiveness of quantity demanded of a good or service to changes in its price.

Overseas trips are elastic in nature because there are many substitutes for overseas trips. Overseas trips are a luxury and they take a high proportion of income.

If the price of overseas trips falls by 4% total revenue will increase because the given fall in price causes a more than proportionate change in quantity demanded.

SELF-EVALUATION REVIEW

Tick (✔) which of the following you know the precise economic answers to (go back and learn those that you have not ticked).

	(✔) TICK
Calculate price elasticity of demand either using the midpoint method or relating it to total expenditure.	☐
Recognise the reasons for differing price elasticities of demand for various goods.	☐
Appreciate that some firms will use the concepts of elasticity of demand in their pricing decisions of goods and services.	☐

5 CROSS ELASTICITY OF DEMAND, ECROSS AND INCOME ELASTICITY OF DEMAND, EY

Key concepts and terms: cross elasticity of demand, calculation of cross elasticity of demand, income elasticity of demand, calculation of income elasticity of demand, significance for firms of income elasticity or cross elasticity of demand (3.3).

SUBSTITUTES OR COMPLEMENTS

Cross elasticity of demand (Ecross) measures the responsiveness of the quantity demanded of one good to changes in the price of another good.

Cross elasticity can be used to understand and classify the relationships between goods and services, it can indicate if products are substitutes or complements simply by the sign of the coefficient. A positive cross elasticity coefficient indicates that the products are substitutes while a negative coefficient indicates they are complements.

The formulas used in calculating cross elasticity of demand are somewhat similar to those used in calculating price elasticity of demand, and are employed following the same principles. Commodities are labelled simply as X and Y (or A and B).

Midpoint method

$$\text{Ecross} = \frac{\left(\dfrac{\text{change in quantity demanded of X}}{\text{midpoint of quantity demanded of X given}}\right)}{\left(\dfrac{\text{change in price of Y}}{\text{midpoint of the prices of Y indicated}}\right)} = \frac{\left(\dfrac{\Delta QX}{\dfrac{QX_1 + QX_2}{2}}\right)}{\left(\dfrac{\Delta PY}{\dfrac{PY_1 + PY_2}{2}}\right)}$$

For example: The purchases of good X increased from 100 to 150 units as the price of good Y decreased from \$100 to \$80.

$$\text{Ecross} = \frac{\left(\dfrac{\text{change in quantity demanded of X}}{\text{midpoint of quantity demanded of X given}}\right)}{\left(\dfrac{\text{change in price of Y}}{\text{midpoint of the prices of Y indicated}}\right)} = \frac{\left(\dfrac{50}{125}\right)}{\left(\dfrac{-20}{90}\right)} = -1.80$$

goods X and Y are complements because the Ecross is a negative coefficient

Percentage change method

$$\text{Ecross} = \frac{\%\Delta QD\,(A)}{\%\Delta P\,(B)}$$

where
Ecross = coefficient of cross elasticity of demand
%ΔQD (A) = percentage change in quantity demanded of commodity A
%ΔP (B) = percentage change in price of commodity B

For example: The price of good B fell by 8% and as a result the purchases of good A decreased by 20%.

$$\text{Ecross} = \frac{\%\Delta QD\,(A)}{\%\Delta P\,(B)} = \frac{-20\%}{-8\%} = +2.50$$

goods A and B are substitutes because the Ecross is a positive coefficient

The size of the coefficient will indicate the strength of the relationship. A coefficient between zero and one denotes weak cross elasticity, while figures greater than 1 imply a close relationship and strong cross elasticity.

ISBN 9780170241212
ISBN 9780170241229

Substitutes are products that can be used in place of something else, for example, butter in place of margarine, coffee in place of tea, beef in place of lamb. For substitutes a rise in the price of one good and thus an increase in demand for the substitute (alternative) is a positive change. This is shown in the graphs. This is a positive change because price and demand for these products move in the same direction, which means that the products are substitutes.

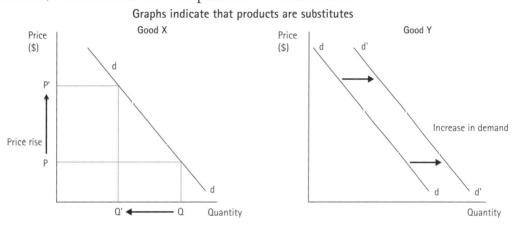

Complements are products that go or are used together, for example, cars and petrol, hot dogs and tomato sauce. For a complement the rise in price of one causes a decrease in demand for the other, a negative change. The effect on graphs is shown below. This is a negative change because price and demand for these products move in opposite directions indicating that the products are complements.

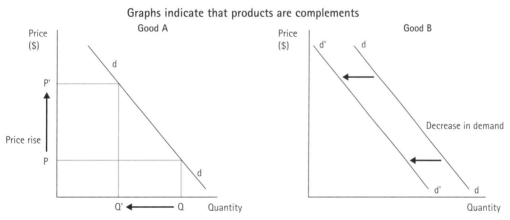

INCOME ELASTICITY OF DEMAND, EY

Income elasticity of demand (Ey) measures the *responsiveness of quantity demanded to changes in consumer incomes.*

Income elasticity of demand is concerned with the way in which consumer demand responds to a change in income. The coefficient of income elasticity of demand will determine if the good or service is inferior, normal necessities or normal luxuries.

An **inferior good** is a good or service for which the quantity demanded and income changes move in opposite directions, and income elasticity (Ey) is a negative number. We buy less inferior goods and services as our income rises.

A **normal good** is a good or service for which changes in quantity demanded and income move in the same direction, for example if income increases so will quantity demanded. Income elasticity for a normal necessity is greater than zero but less than one; for a normal luxury the income elasticity is greater than one. In both cases, for a normal good the income elasticity is a positive number.

To calculate income elasticity of demand we use the following formulas:

Percentage change method

$$Ey = \frac{\%\Delta QD}{\%\Delta Y}$$

where

Ey = income elasticity of demand
$\%\Delta QD$ = percentage change in quantity demanded
$\%\Delta Y$ = percentage change in consumers' income

For example: Julian's income rises by 4% and the quantity decreases by 10%.

$$Ey = \frac{\%\Delta QD}{\%\Delta Y} = \frac{-10\%}{4\%} = -2.50 \text{ inferior good}$$

Income and quantity changes are in opposite directions so Ey is a negative number.

Midpoint method

$$Ey = \frac{\left(\dfrac{\text{change in quantity demanded}}{\text{midpoint of quantity demanded}}\right)}{\left(\dfrac{\text{change in income}}{\text{midpoint of incomes}}\right)} = \frac{\left(\dfrac{\Delta Q}{\dfrac{Q1 + Q2}{2}}\right)}{\left(\dfrac{\Delta Y}{\dfrac{Y1 + Y2}{2}}\right)}$$

For example: Bill's income fell from \$200 to \$150 and quantity demanded decreases from 50 to 40.

$$Ey = \frac{\left(\dfrac{\text{change in quantity demanded}}{\text{midpoint of quantity demanded}}\right)}{\left(\dfrac{\text{change in income}}{\text{midpoint of incomes}}\right)} = \frac{\left(\dfrac{-10}{45}\right)}{\left(\dfrac{-50}{175}\right)} = 0.78 \text{ normal necessity}$$

Both income and quantity fell for Bill so since these changes are in the same direction, Ey is a positive number which indicates a normal good.

Firms would respond to increasing incomes in a society by producing more normal goods and fewer inferior products. During a recession with falling incomes and people losing jobs, products with high income elasticity of demand (normal luxuries) will be most affected because people will be forced to buy other products (necessities or inferior goods).

KEY TERMS AND IDEAS

Cross elasticity of demand	Measures the responsiveness of quantity demanded of one good to changes in price of another good. Cross elasticity can indicate if goods are substitutes or complements
Substitutes	Ecross is a positive coefficient
Complements	Ecross is a negative coefficient
Income elasticity of demand (Ey)	Measures the responsiveness of quantity demanded to changes in incomes.
Inferior goods	Ey is a negative number. Quantity demanded and income changes are in opposite directions.
Normal goods	Ey is a positive number. Quantity demanded and income changes are in the same direction. If Ey > 1, the commodity is a normal luxury. If 0 < Ey < 1, the commodity is a normal necessity.

CROSS ELASTICITY OF DEMAND, ECROSS AND INCOME ELASTICITY OF DEMAND, Ey

ISBN 9780170241212
ISBN 9780170241229

STUDENT NOTES: CROSS ELASTICITY AND INCOME ELASTICITY OF DEMAND

<u>Income elasticity of demand (Ey)</u> – measures the responsiveness of quantity demanded of a good (or service) to changes in consumers' incomes.

<u>Income elasticity of demand coefficient</u> – used to classify goods, if positive as a normal good, or if negative an inferior good.

<u>Normal luxuries</u> – Ey > 1, e.g., overseas trips, fashion clothing, will be most affected in times of a recession.

<u>Normal necessities</u> – Ey < 1, i.e., basic commodities, e.g., salt, bread, milk.

<u>Inferior goods</u> – Ey a negative coefficient (less than zero), i.e., the quantity demanded will actually fall as income rises, e.g., cheap cuts of meat, secondhand clothes.

<u>Cross elasticity of demand (Ecross)</u> – measures the responsiveness of quantity demanded of one good, to changes in the price of another good.

<u>Cross elasticity of demand coefficient</u> – used to classify the relationship between goods and services as substitutes (a positive coefficient) or complements (a negative coefficient).

<u>Complements</u> – products that are used in conjunction with one another, e.g., movie tickets and popcorn. As the price of movie tickets increase the quantity demanded decreases and the demand for popcorn will decrease. Therefore, Ecross is a negative relationship

<u>Substitutes</u> – products that are used in place of each other, e.g., catching train or bus to work. As the price of train trips increase the quantity demanded decreases and demand for bus rides will increase as it is relatively cheaper. Therefore, Ecross is a positive change.

PRACTISE QUESTIONS AND TASKS

1 a Define 'cross elasticity of demand'.

Measures the responsiveness of quantity demanded of one good to changes in price of another good.

b What is the purpose of calculating cross elasticity of demand?

Cross elasticity can be used to understand and classify the relationship between goods or services, it can determine if products are substitutes or complements.

c Calculate cross elasticity of demand and indicate if the products are substitutes or complements.

(i) The price of good A increased by 8% and the quantity demanded of good B rose by 5%.

$$Ecross = \frac{\left(\dfrac{0.05}{0.08}\right)}{} = +0.63 \text{ substitutes}$$

(ii) The price of good A rose from \$8 to \$12 and in response the purchases for good B decreased from 200 units to 100 units.

$$Ecross = \frac{\left(\dfrac{-100}{150}\right)}{\left(\dfrac{4}{10}\right)} = -1.667 = -1.67 \text{ complements}$$

2 Work out the income elasticity for each question using the midpoint method and indicate what type of goods they are. Show your working.

a When an individual's disposable income falls from \$500 to \$450 per week, their purchases of a product increase from 12 to 15.

$$Ey = \frac{\left(\dfrac{+3}{13.5}\right)}{\left(\dfrac{-50}{475}\right)} = -2.11 \quad \text{inferior good}$$

b

Previous income	\$40 000
New income	\$50 000
Previous purchases	100
New purchases	120

$$Ey = \frac{\left(\dfrac{20}{110}\right)}{\left(\dfrac{10\,000}{45\,000}\right)} = 0.818 = 0.82 \quad \text{normal necessity}$$

c

	Quantity demanded	Income (\$)
New situation	4	30
Old situation	8	40

$$Ey = \frac{\left(\dfrac{-4}{6}\right)}{\left(\dfrac{-10}{35}\right)} = 2.333 = 2.33 \quad \text{normal luxury}$$

ISBN 9780170241212
ISBN 9780170241229

3 **a** Define 'income elasticity' and give the formula to calculate Ey.

<u>Measures the responsiveness of quantity demanded to changes in a consumer's/individual's income.</u>

$$Ey = \frac{\left(\dfrac{\Delta QD}{midpt\ QD}\right)}{\left(\dfrac{\Delta Y}{midpt\ Y}\right)}$$

b Complete the table.

	Information	Inferior goods Normal necessities Normal luxuries
(i)	Income and quantity demanded changes are in opposite directions	inferior goods
(ii)	Goods have a negative income elasticity of demand	inferior goods
(iii)	Goods have a positive income elasticity of demand	normal luxuries/necessities
(iv)	Ey < 0	inferior goods
(v)	An increase in incomes leads to an increase in demand (or quantity demanded)	normal luxuries/necessities
(vi)	Income elasticity of demand is greater than one	normal luxury
(vii)	An increase in income will cause quantity demanded to decrease	inferior goods
(viii)	A drop in income will cause a decrease in demand	normal necessities/luxuries
(ix)	If a household's income rose from $200 to $250 per week and the quantity demanded rose from 20 to 24	$\dfrac{\left(\frac{4}{22}\right)}{\left(\frac{50}{225}\right)} = \dfrac{0.18}{0.22} = 0.82$ normal necessities
(x)	If a household's income rose from $200 to $250 per week and the quantity demanded fell from 24 to 20	$\dfrac{\left(\frac{-4}{22}\right)}{\left(\frac{50}{225}\right)} = -0.82$ inferior goods
(xi)	The percentage change in income brings about a much larger percentage change in quantity demanded, e.g., laptop computer, cellphones	normal luxuries
(xii)	A percentage fall in income causes only a small percentage decrease in quantity demanded, e.g., salt, bread	normal necessities
(xiii)	A percentage rise in income causes a percentage decrease in quantity demanded.	inferior goods

c Complete the empty spaces in the sentences below.

Income elasticity of demand (Ey) <u>measures</u> the <u>responsiveness</u> of

quantity demanded to <u>changes in consumers' income</u>. Goods and

services with a negative income elasticity of demand are classified as <u>inferior goods</u>.

Goods and services with a <u>positive income elasticity of demand</u> are

classified as normal goods.

PHOTOCOPYING PROHIBITED   ISBN 9780170241212   ISBN 9780170241229   Cross elasticity of demand, Ecross and income elasticity of demand, Ey   **41**

4 a An economist planned to measure the strength of a possible relationship between increasing diesel prices and the quantity of alternative fuels demanded. Name the elasticity concept that would be used.

Cross elasticity of demand.

b Complete the table by placing a tick (✓) in the column to indicate the cross elasticity of demand coefficient.

Situation	Positive coefficient	Negative coefficient
(i) A rise in the price of one good causes a fall in the quantity of the other good.		✓
(ii) A rise in the price of one good causes a rise in the quantity of the other good.	✓	
(iii) A fall in the price of one good causes a fall in the quantity of the other good.	✓	

c Define cross elasticity of demand.

Measures the responsiveness of quantity demanded of one good to changes in price of another good.

5 The consumption of apples declined by 12% and the consumption of oranges declined by 8%. In the same period, the consumption of bananas increased by 6%.
Assume that the prices of apples and oranges rose by 4% over the same period of time.

a (i) Calculate the coefficient for the price elasticity of demand for apples. Show your working.

$$Ep = \frac{(-0.12)}{(0.04)} = 3$$

(ii) Assume that the coefficient calculated in a (i) is correct. What has happened to the total revenue of apple producers?

TR will fall.

b (i) Calculate the coefficient for the price elasticity of demand for bananas to a change in price of apples. Show your working.

$$Ecross = \frac{(0.06)}{(0.04)} = 1.5$$

(ii) What does your answer to b (i) suggest about the relationship between bananas and apples?

Apples and bananas are substitutes.

ISBN 9780170241212
ISBN 9780170241229

REVIEW QUESTIONS

1 Pizzas and gourmet hamburgers are substitutes, while a rented DVD would be considered a complement for either a pizza or gourmet burger.

Explain cross elasticity of demand and price elasticity of demand. In your answer you should:

- Indicate if the cross elasticity of demand for pizzas and gourmet hamburgers is a positive or negative and explain why.
- Explain whether it is a good idea for the firm to raise the price of a good that is inelastic in nature.
- Explain why goods that have no close substitutes have inelastic demand.

The cross-elasticity coefficient for pizzas and gourmet hamburgers is positive because the increase/decrease in the price of one commodity causes an increase/decrease in the demand for the other because they are substitutes.

It is a good idea for a firm to raise price if the good is inelastic in nature because raising the price will cause a less than proportionate fall in quantity demanded so total revenue will rise.

Goods that have no substitute have inelastic demand because if price rises, people have to keep buying this good because there are no substitutes therefore consumption of the good will reduce by proportionately less than the rise in price indicating inelastic demand.

2 Economists can measure the relationship between prices of one product and demand for another. Explain the concept of cross elasticity of demand. In your answer you should:

- Define cross elasticity of demand and indicate what the cross elasticity coefficient indicates.
- Explain with the aid of a diagram what substitutes are.
- Explain with the aid of a diagram what complements are.

Cross elasticity of demand (Ecross) measures the responsiveness of the quantity demanded of one good to changes in the price of another good.

Cross elasticity can indicate if products are substitutes or complements simply by the sign of the coefficient. A positive cross elasticity coefficient indicates that the products are substitutes while a negative coefficient indicates they are complements.

Substitutes are products that can be used in place of something else, for example, butter in place of margarine, coffee in place of tea, beef in place of lamb. For substitutes a rise in the price of one good and thus an increase in demand for the substitute (alternative) is a positive change. This is shown in the graphs. This is a positive change because price and demand for these products move in the same direction, which means that the products are substitutes.

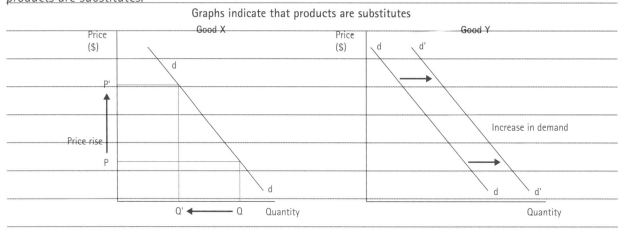

Graphs indicate that products are substitutes

Complements are products that go or are used together, for example, cars and petrol, hot dogs and tomato sauce. For a complement the rise in price of one causes a decrease in demand for the other, a negative change. The effect on graphs is shown below. This is a negative change because price and demand for these products move in opposite directions indicating that the products are complements.

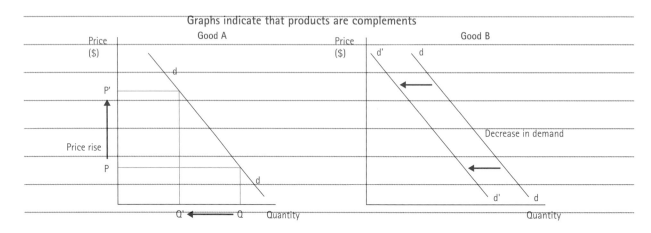

Graphs indicate that products are complements

ISBN 9780170241212
ISBN 9780170241229

3   Income elasticity of demand is used by firms when making decisions.
Explain income elasticity of demand. In your answer you should:

- Explain income elasticity of demand.
- Explain the difference between inferior and normal goods.
- Explain how a firm's knowledge of income elasticity will influence its decision making.

Income elasticity of demand measures the responsiveness of quantity demanded to changes in consumer
incomes.

Income elasticity of demand is concerned with the way in which consumer demand responds to a change in
income. The coefficient of income elasticity of demand will determine if the good or service is inferior, a normal
necessity or a normal luxury.

An inferior good is a good or service for which the quantity demanded and income changes move in opposite
directions, and income elasticity (Ey) is a negative number. Individuals buy less inferior goods and services as
income rises.

A normal good is a good or service for which changes in quantity demanded and income move in the same
direction, for example if income increases so will quantity demanded. Income elasticity for a normal necessity
is greater than zero but less than one; for a normal luxury the income elasticity is greater than one. In both
cases, for a normal good the income elasticity is a positive number.

Firms would respond to increasing incomes in a society by producing more normal goods and fewer inferior
products. During a recession with falling incomes and people losing jobs, products with high income elasticity
of demand (normal luxuries) will be most affected because people will be forced to buy other products
(necessities or inferior goods).

SELF-EVALUATION REVIEW

Tick (✔) which of the following you know the precise economic answers to (go back and learn those
that you have not ticked).

	(✔) TICK
Define 'cross elasticity of demand' and calculate cross elasticity of demand and determine if products are substitutes or complements.	☐
Define income elasticity and calculate income elasticity.	☐
Explain the relationship between the level of individual incomes and the type of goods and services they are likely to purchase.	☐

Key concepts and terms: price elasticity of supply, calculation of price elasticity of supply, supply responsiveness in the long term compared with the short term (3.3).

Price elasticity of supply (Es) measures the *responsiveness of quantity supplied of a good to changes in price*.

To calculate the coefficient of price elasticity of supply we divide the percentage change in quantity supplied by the percentage change in price. The formula is given below.

Percentage change method

$$Es = \frac{\%\Delta QS}{\%\Delta P}$$
where
Es = coefficient of price elasticity of supply
$\%\Delta QS$ = percentage change in quantity supplied
$\%\Delta P$ = percentage change in price

When Es > 1 the price elasticity of supply is termed elastic.
When Es = 1 the price elasticity of supply is termed unitary.
When Es < 1 the price elasticity of supply is termed inelastic.

For example, as the price of the product increased by 8% the quantity supplied increased by 5%.

$$Es = \frac{\%\Delta QS}{\%\Delta P} = \frac{5\%}{8\%} = 0.63 \text{ supply is inelastic}$$

Midpoint method
Price elasticity of supply can be calculated by the midpoint method as shown.

$$Es = \frac{\left(\dfrac{\text{change in quantity supplied}}{\text{midpoint of quantity supplied given}}\right)}{\left(\dfrac{\text{change in price}}{\text{midpoint of the prices indicated}}\right)} = \frac{\left(\dfrac{\Delta Qs}{\dfrac{Q1 + Q2}{2}}\right)}{\left(\dfrac{\Delta P}{\dfrac{P1 + P2}{2}}\right)}$$

For example, at a price of $110 quantity supplied is 500, while at a price of $90 quantity supplied is 300.

$$Es = \frac{\left(\dfrac{\text{change in quantity supplied}}{\text{midpoint of quantity supplied given}}\right)}{\left(\dfrac{\text{change in price}}{\text{midpoint of the prices indicated}}\right)} = \frac{\left(\dfrac{200}{400}\right)}{\left(\dfrac{20}{100}\right)} = 2.50 \quad \text{supply is elastic}$$

In extreme cases slope will indicate the price elasticity of supply.

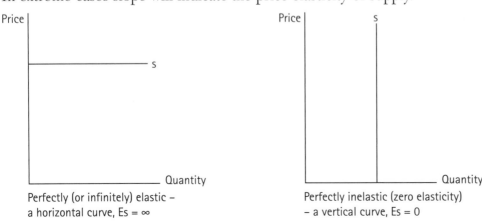

Perfectly (or infinitely) elastic –
a horizontal curve, Es = ∞

Perfectly inelastic (zero elasticity)
– a vertical curve, Es = 0

ISBN 9780170241212
ISBN 9780170241229

INELASTIC AND ELASTIC SUPPLY

When price elasticity of supply is less than one this means that a given change in price causes a less than proportionate change in quantity supplied and indicates inelastic supply.

When price elasticity of supply is greater than one this means that a given change in price causes a more than proportionate change in quantity supplied and indicates elastic supply.

SUPPLY OVER TIME

Supply is inelastic, or relatively unresponsive to price changes in the short run, and elastic, or relatively responsive, in the long run.

In the **short-run time period**, at least one input is fixed. The firm is restricted in its ability to change output. In the short run the supply of all goods is inelastic because the quantity supplied is limited to the quantity of finished goods on hand or easily available. Supply elasticity is said to be lower.

In the **long run** firms have time to expand their use of *all* factors and so increase their total output capacity. Shortages and profits will attract more firms to the industry, which will increase total market supply. Over time, supply will be more responsive to price (elastic) as existing producers are able to increase production levels, new producers can enter the market, and improvements in technology increase productivity. Elasticity is then said to be higher.

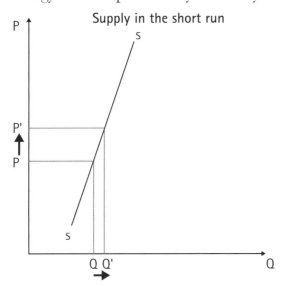

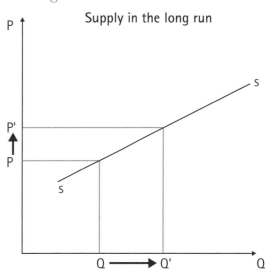

In response to a price change output will change by more in the long-run than short-run time period, as shown in the two diagrams.

Momentary supply is supply at this moment in time and is sometimes referred to as supply on a given day when quantity supplied is fixed regardless of price.

This is illustrated by the perfectly inelastic supply curve shown, drawn as a vertical line.

The curve reflects that firms have only a fixed amount of stock on hand available to meet demand and are unable to alter any factors, for example tickets to a school social, or the lots available for sale at an auction.

There is no responsiveness in the quantity supplied to a change in price and the coefficient of elasticity of supply is zero.

KEY TERMS AND IDEAS

Price elasticity of supply (Es)	Measures the responsiveness of quantity supplied of a good to changes in its price
Formula to calculate price elasticity of supply, midpoint method Es > 1, elastic Es = 1, unitary Es < 1, inelastic	$$Es = \frac{\left(\dfrac{\text{change in quantity supplied}}{\text{midpoint of quantity supplied given}}\right)}{\left(\dfrac{\text{change in price}}{\text{midpoint of the prices indicated}}\right)} = \frac{\left(\dfrac{\Delta Qs}{\dfrac{Q1 + Q2}{2}}\right)}{\left(\dfrac{\Delta P}{\dfrac{P1 + P2}{2}}\right)}$$
Inelastic supply (Es < 1)	A given change in price causes a less than proportionate change in quantity supplied.
Elastic supply (Es > 1)	A given change in price causes a more than proportionate change in quantity supplied.
Momentary time period (or supply on a given day) Short-run supply Long-run supply	The quantity supplied is fixed and cannot respond to changes in price; the curve is drawn as a vertical line and is perfectly inelastic. Firms are unable to change any inputs (factors). At least one input is fixed and therefore the firm is restricted in its ability to change supply/output levels. Supply in the short run will be more inelastic (or lower) and less elastic. All inputs are variable therefore the firm can be more adaptable and more efficient. Supply is more elastic (or higher) and less inelastic in the long run.

ISBN 9780170241212
ISBN 9780170241229

STUDENT NOTES: PRICE ELASTICITY OF SUPPLY, Es

Price elasticity of supply (Es) – measures the responsiveness of quantity supplied of a good or service to a change in its price.

Price elasticity of supply coefficient – enables us to classify supply curves as inelastic (Es < 1) or elastic (Es > 1) which helps us understand the response a firm will have to a change in price for its output.

Momentary supply – (perfectly inelastic supply Es = 0) supply curve is drawn as a vertical line this is because there can be no responsiveness in the quantity supplied to a change in price. The quantity supplied is fixed.

Short-run supply – (relatively inelastic) firms have at least one fixed factor and therefore the firm is restricted in its ability to change supply/output levels. Supply in the short run will be lower or more inelastic.

Long-run supply – (relatively elastic) firms can alter all factors therefore firms can be adaptable, supply is higher or more elastic.

Inelastic supply – (Es < 1) a given increase in price evokes a less than proportionate increase in quantity supplied.

Elastic supply – (Es > 1) a given increase in price evokes a more than proportionate increase in quantity supplied.

PRACTISE QUESTIONS AND TASKS

1 a Define 'price elasticity of supply'.

Measures the responsiveness of the quantity supplied of a good to a change in its price.

b Work out the price elasticity of supply for each question below (show your working). Use the midpoint method.

(i)

Price ($)	Quantity supplied
1.00	17
0.95	10

$$Es = \frac{\left(\frac{-7}{13.5}\right)}{\left(\frac{-0.05}{0.975}\right)} = 10.11 \text{ elastic}$$

(ii)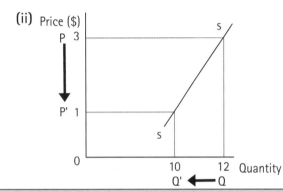

$$Es = \frac{\left(\frac{-2}{11}\right)}{\left(\frac{-2}{2}\right)} = 0.18 \text{ inelastic}$$

c Use the diagram to match up the curves with the description below. Write the letter of your choice.

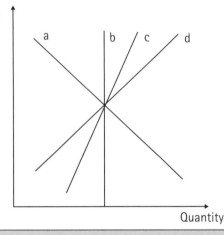

Relatively inelastic supply	c
Demand curve	a
Momentary supply curve – on a given day	b
Relatively elastic supply	d

d Describe the price elasticity of supply indicated by the situations outlined in the table below.

Situation		Elasticity
(i)	The response to a given change in price is a more than proportionate change in quantity supplied.	Elastic supply
(ii)	The response to a given change in price is a less than proportionate change in quantity supplied.	Inelastic supply
(iii)	A given price change causes no change in quantity supplied.	Perfectly inelastic
(iv)	%Δ price > %Δ quantity supplied	Inelastic supply
(v)	%Δ quantity supplied > %Δ price	Elastic supply

ISBN 9780170241212
ISBN 9780170241229

2 Calculate the price elasticity of supply for each question below (show your working). Use the midpoint method.

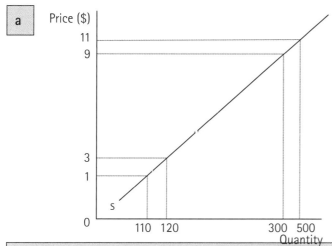

a Price ($)

(i) Between $11 and $9:

$$Es = \frac{\left(\dfrac{200}{400}\right)}{\left(\dfrac{-2}{10}\right)} = 2.50 \text{ elastic}$$

(ii) Between $3 and $1:

$$Es = \frac{\left(\dfrac{-10}{115}\right)}{\left(\dfrac{-2}{2}\right)} = 0.09 \text{ inelastic}$$

b Briefly explain why there is a difference in the short-run and long-run supply curves for bottled water.

Idea that supply can adjust in response to situations over a period of time. In the short run there is at least one fixed factor of production and therefore the firm is restricted in its ability to change supply/output levels. In the long run all inputs can be varied, therefore the firms can be more adaptable and more efficient in the production of bottled water.

c What is the price elasticity of supply when quantity supplied increases from 10 to 12 as the price increases from $200 to $250? Show your working.

$$Es = \frac{\left(\dfrac{2}{11}\right)}{\left(\dfrac{50}{225}\right)} = 0.82 \text{ inelastic}$$

d Define 'supply elasticity' and give the formula to calculate Es.

The responsiveness of the quantity supplied of a good to a change in its price.

$$Es = \frac{\left(\dfrac{\Delta QS}{\text{midpt QS}}\right)}{\left(\dfrac{\Delta P}{\text{midpt P}}\right)}$$

3 Below are the correct supply curves in the short-run and long-run time periods. Use these graphs and your own knowledge to complete the sentences that follow.

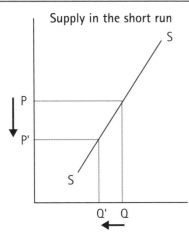

Supply in the short run

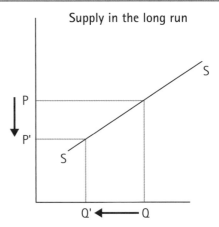

Supply in the long run

| a | Supply in the short run is relatively <u>inelastic</u> and in the long run relatively <u>elastic</u>.

| b | 'In response to a price d<u>ecrease</u> the output will fall by more in the <u>long</u> run than

it does in the <u>short</u> run.'

| c | In the short run supply is relatively unr<u>esponsive</u> and in the long run more <u>responsive</u>.

| d | Supply on a given day is p<u>erfectly</u> <u>inelastic</u> and the curve is drawn

as a <u>vertical</u> line.

| e | When a given price change causes a more than proportionate change in quantity supplied this indicates

<u>elastic supply</u>. The short-run supply curve is relatively <u>inelastic</u>.

| f | Inelastic supply occurs when a given change <u>in price causes a less than proportionate change in quantity</u>

<u>supplied</u>. The long-run supply is relatively e<u>lastic</u>.

4 Calculate price elasticity of supply for each question below (show your working). Use the midpoint method.

| a |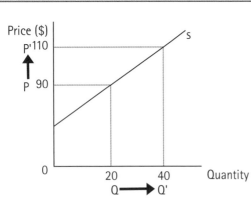

$$Es = \dfrac{\left(\dfrac{20}{30}\right)}{\left(\dfrac{20}{100}\right)} = 3.33 \text{ elastic}$$

| b |

Price ($)	Quantity supplied
1.00	30
1.50	34

$$Es = \dfrac{\left(\dfrac{+4}{32}\right)}{\left(\dfrac{+.50}{1.25}\right)} = 0.31 \text{ inelastic}$$

ISBN 9780170241212
ISBN 9780170241229

PHOTOCOPYING PROHIBITED

REVIEW QUESTIONS

1 **Supply over time**

Supply is inelastic, or relatively unresponsive to price changes in the short run, and elastic, or relatively responsive, in the long run.

Explain supply over time. In your answer you should use diagrams and:

- Explain the momentary time period.
- Explain the short-run time period.
- Explain the long-run time period.

Momentary supply is supply at this moment in time and is sometimes referred to as supply on a given day when quantity supplied is fixed regardless of price.

This is illustrated by the perfectly inelastic supply curve shown, drawn as a vertical line.

The curve reflects that firms have only a fixed amount of stock on hand available to meet demand and are unable to alter any factors, for example tickets to a school social, or the lots available for sale at an auction.

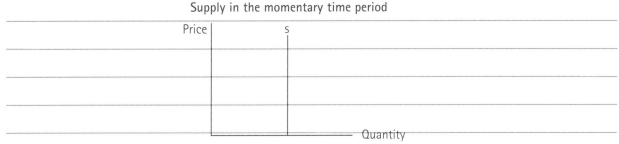

Supply in the momentary time period

In the short-run time period, at least one input is fixed. The firm is restricted in its ability to change output.

In the short run the supply of all goods is inelastic because the quantity supplied is limited to the quantity of finished goods on hand or easily available. Supply elasticity is said to be lower.

In the long run firms have time to expand their use of all factors and so increase their total output capacity. Shortages and profits will attract more firms to the industry, which will increase total market supply. Over time, supply will be more responsive to price (elastic) as existing producers are able to increase production levels, new producers can enter the market, and improvements in technology increase productivity. Elasticity is then said to be higher.

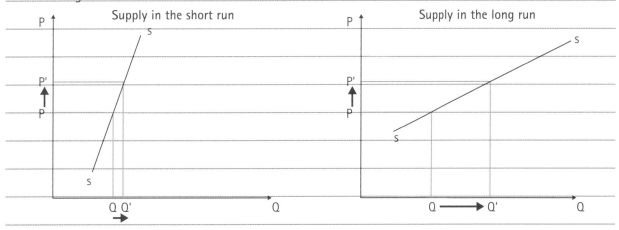

In response to a price change output will change by more in the long-run than short-run time period, as shown in the two diagrams.

2 Alfred Marshall developed the economic theory that price elasticity of supply for a good or service is linked to time periods.

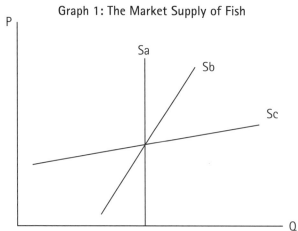

Graph 1: The Market Supply of Fish

Explain price elasticity of supply. In your answer you should:

- Define price elasticity of supply and explain the difference between inelastic and elastic supply.
- Assume that fish prices have increased. With reference to Graph 1, explain which of the three supply curves for fish is most appropriate for a period of one year. Justify your answer.

Price elasticity of supply measures the responsiveness of quantity supplied of a good or service to a change in its price.

When price elasticity of supply is less than one this means that a given change in price causes a less than proportionate change in quantity supplied and indicates inelastic supply.

When price elasticity of supply is greater than one this means that a given change in price causes a more than proportionate change in quantity supplied and indicates elastic supply.

The most appropriate supply curve for a year is Sb (or Sc).

Sb – idea that there is some ability to increase supply of fish in one year/some inputs are variable, others are fixed. Sc – idea that in the longer run all inputs are variable.

SELF-EVALUATION REVIEW

Tick (✔) which of the following you know the precise economic answers to (go back and learn those that you have not ticked).

	(✔) TICK
Define 'price elasticity of supply'.	☐
Calculate price elasticity of supply.	☐
Explain why supply is more responsive in the long run than in the short run.	☐
Apply the concept of elasticity of supply in a given situation.	☐

ISBN 9780170241212
ISBN 9780170241229

7   ROLE OF PRICES AND PROFITS

Key concepts and terms: sunrise and sunset industries (3.3).

SUNRISE AND SUNSET INDUSTRIES

A firm is a single business while an industry is the sum of all firms which produce one type of product. The dairy industry in New Zealand includes all those firms involved in producing dairy products for sale from the farmers who milk cows, firms who process the milk into final or intermediate products, and firms who market the final product.

If prices for dairy products in world markets rise, the industry as a whole will prosper and grow. Dairy farmers will be encouraged to invest more in milk production. For example, farmers may purchase land, converting sheep farms to dairy production. This will involve the purchase of capital items such as milking sheds, tractors and equipment. Milk production will increase, farmers' incomes will rise and they may employ extra workers.

Factories processing milk and firms marketing the final product will also increase output and sales. Employment will rise and spending will increase beyond the dairy industry.

The hospitality and travel industry may well benefit as individuals with increased disposable incomes take holidays and travel. Regions whose economies are dependent on the dairy industry are likely to benefit the most from the expansion in economic activity.

As domestic and global economies go through the trade cycle of recession, recovery and boom, it is likely that the part of the trade cycle that the New Zealand economy is in will differ from a number of its trading partners. If there is a downturn in overseas demand, there are likely to be reduced incomes and possibly business closures for firms that rely heavily on export orders. Unemployment is likely to rise and living standards in the affected areas and communities will be lower.

The converse applies for a recovery and increase in overseas demand. While some industries may be experiencing a decline in activities it is possible that other industries are experiencing growth, e.g., while the car and shoe manufacturing industries have declined, other industries such as tourism, wine, education and dairying have grown in size and importance in the New Zealand economy.

The changing demand for a product in local or world markets may be temporary or permanent. Resources will switch from declining industries (**sunset**) into growth industries (**sunrise**) where prospects and profits are likely to be better.

There is always likely to be a change in the fortune of various industries within an economy at any given point in time. The change will mean some individuals losing jobs in some industries, while new opportunities arise in other industries, some firms' profits declining while others are growing, firms may close down or may go through a process of restructuring.

KEY TERMS AND IDEAS

Firm	A single business.
Industry	The sum of all firms which produce one type of product.
Sunrise industry	A growth (expanding) industry where prospects and profits are likely to be improving.
Sunset industry	A declining industry where resources will be shifted away into other industries where their prospects are better and the returns to the owners are higher.

ISBN 9780170241212
ISBN 9780170241229

STUDENT NOTES: ROLE OF PRICES AND PROFITS

An increase in sales and revenue will encourage New Zealand firms to increase production as stock levels fall. To satisfy the increase in demand firms will need to hire additional workers or pay existing workers overtime. An increase in business confidence will mean that firms will invest in new capital. Resources may switch out of less profitable ventures/industries and into growth industries, for example, the growth of the dairying industry.

New Zealand firms import products because the price is lower than the New Zealand price. As New Zealand firms import goods and services, local (domestic) firms must match the world (overseas) price or lose sales. As the price falls, some domestic producers may be unable to cover the costs of production so decide to close down or produce another good or service. The fall in price will cause the quantity demanded in the local market to increase.

A firm's profit depends on earning revenue from sales while keeping costs as low as possible.

ISBN 9780170241212
ISBN 9780170241229

PRACTISE QUESTIONS AND TASKS

> Government economic reform and changes in domestic and international demand patterns have transformed the New Zealand economy. Businesses have shifted from old 'sunset' industries to innovative 'sunrise' industries.

1 a Indicate if the following industries are 'sunset' or 'sunrise' industries.

(i)	boat building	sunrise	(ii)	organics	sunrise
(iii)	car manufacturing	sunset	(iv)	wine	sunrise
(v)	education	sunrise	(vi)	tourism	sunrise
(vii)	film making	sunrise	(viii)	shoe manufacturing	sunset
(ix)	dairying	sunrise	(x)	wool and sheep	sunset

b The difficulty with economic reform is the short-term losses, and long-run gains. Outline some possible short-term losses and long-run gains that were a result of from reform policies that liberalised trade in New Zealand.

(i) Short-term losses: Idea of businesses making less profit or closing down, workers made redundant, unemployment and the lowering of standards of living in the affected communities and areas.

(ii) Long-term gains: Idea of more efficient resource use, development of new industries and new employment opportunities as sunrise industries develop.

c Indicate if the following statements are facts or opinions. Justify your answers.

(i) A 'sunset' industry will always be a 'sunset' industry.   opinion
Justification: While an industry may be in decline for a certain time period, demand domestically and internationally may change and cause a sunset industry to grow at a later date.

(ii) The growth and contraction of some New Zealand industries will depend on what goes on in the global economy.   fact
Justification: New Zealand is part of a worldwide (global) economy with exports contributing 30% to New Zealand GDP. Recessions and booms in overseas economies and changes in international demand will therefore impact on many New Zealand industries. For some industries it will mean contraction while for others expansion.

ISBN 9780170241212
ISBN 9780170241229
ROLE OF PRICES AND PROFITS

2 a **(i)** Complete the table to indicate if the following event or situation will result in growth or contraction of industries.

(ii) Complete the table with a tick (✓) to indicate which industries are likely to be affected by the situation or event outlined.

Situation or event	Growth or contraction of industries	Education industry	Tourism industry	Marine industry	Farming (agriculture/ horticulture) industry
New Zealand wins the Americas Cup.	growth		✓	✓	
An outbreak of mad cow disease in Europe and America.	growth				✓
A SARS outbreak in Asia and downturn in Asian economies.	contraction	✓	✓	✓	✓
A reduction in quotas and tariffs on New Zealand-made products by the European Union.	growth				✓

b Complete the table with a tick (✓) to indicate if the situation outlined is likely to occur when the economy is expanding or contracting.

Situation		Expanding economy	Contracting economy
(i)	A rise in the number of business closures.		✓
(ii)	A decrease in the number of building consents.		✓
(iii)	An increase in the level of business confidence.	✓	
(iv)	Workers are being made redundant and levels of unemployment are rising.		✓
(v)	Firms are paying workers overtime and there is a scarcity of resources available.	✓	
(vi)	Increased investment by firms and Real GDP is rising.	✓	
(vii)	Firms are recording record sales and company profits rise.	✓	

c Complete the statements below using the words provided.

consumer	dying	growth	restructured	sunset
declining	dynamic	losing	retrain	Workers
down	expanding	prospects	sunrise	

Markets are <u>dynamic</u>, they are constantly changing as a result of changes in

<u>consumer</u> tastes and preferences. <u>Workers</u> who lose jobs in <u>sunset</u>

industries may need to <u>retrain</u> in skills demanded by the expanding (<u>sunrise</u>)

industries. Resources should reallocate from <u>declining</u> or <u>dying</u> industries (sunset)

to <u>expanding</u> or <u>growth</u> industries (sunrise) where <u>prospects</u> are better. The

change from sunset to sunrise industries will mean some individuals <u>losing</u> jobs, firms

closing <u>down</u> or being <u>restructured</u>.

ISBN 9780170241212
ISBN 9780170241229

3 Read the extract and answer the questions that follow.

> An outbreak of mad cow disease in Europe is predicted to have an impact on the level of economic activity in New Zealand immediately and in the long term. Recent years have seen an increase in global demand for agricultural product.

a List several economic effects on the New Zealand farming industry of mad cow disease in Europe.

Increase production; increased exports; higher incomes; jobs created; an improvement in New Zealand's

current account; inflationary pressures.

b Identify the likely impact on economic growth in New Zealand indicated by the information in the extract.

Economic growth will increase, i.e., real GDP will increase.

c Suggest one possible reason for the 'increasing global demand for agricultural products'.

Increased standards of living / increased incomes. Increase in global population or economic growth.

d Describe what happens in an industry when the industry expands.

Sales increase, revenue increases, profits increase, output increases. Firms expand or carry out investment

plans. Workers are hired or paid overtime. Resources are switched into this industry.

e Explain the effect of the dairy industry success on New Zealand's dairy regions.

Increase in regional growth for those areas associated with dairy, an increase in sales and revenue for

retailers as dairy farmers purchase goods and services. Employment opportunities will increase and people

will be attracted into these regions.

REVIEW QUESTIONS

1 The ski industry continues to grow as more tourists visit during the New Zealand winter.
Explain the impact of the ski industry on the New Zealand economy. In your answer you should:
* Explain the effect of increased tourist numbers on the ski industry in New Zealand.
* Explain the effect on prices and profit.

As tourist numbers increase during the ski season, ski operaters' revenue and profits will increase because of the higher turnover due to the increased demand. Ski operators may have to hire additional staff and train them, or pay existing staff overtime to satisfy the extra demand from increased numbers of tourists. Ski operators may extend the ski season, open up new ski areas or invest in new snow machines, etc. As ski operators become more confident about the future they may borrow funds to invest in plant and machinery to increase profit, because they have higher expectations about the returns and profits they will make.

Increased tourist numbers will cause demand for ski industry goods and services to increase which will increase the price firms receive. Firms are receiving a higher price and the quantity sold has increased, higher revenues will be generated. If the revenue firms receive exceeds the cost to provide the additional services, profits will increase as a result. New firms will be attracted into the tourism industry seeking to earn profit.

ROLE OF PRICES AND PROFITS   ISBN 9780170241212
ISBN 9780170241229

2 Foreign fee-paying student numbers continue to decline as the recession continues and the dollar appreciates.

Explain, using the education industry, the effect on an industry when it is in decline. In your answer you should:

- Explain the effect on providers of education.
- Explain the flow-on effects to other industries, profits and resource use.

When the New Zealand dollar appreciates against other currencies the cost of an education in New Zealand for foreign students increases and is more expensive. Since New Zealand is less price competitive, fee-paying students look for a relatively cheaper option. As fewer students come to New Zealand, providers of education services in New Zealand will hire fewer teachers and support staff and put investment plans on hold. Some firms may find that they generate insufficient revenue and may have to close down or switch resources into producing something else that is more profitable.

Other industries will be affected, such as providers of accommodation, meals and essential services, e.g., health, because of the decrease in demand the profits of these firms are likely to fall as revenue decreases. Firms may decide to switch resources into other activities that are more profitable.

SELF-EVALUATION REVIEW

Tick (✔) which of the following you know the precise economic answers to (go back and learn those that you have not ticked).

	(✔) TICK
Explain the role of prices and profits.	☐